Passages from the Search for Eternal Love

I0103899

Kelly Brown

chipmunkapublishing
the mental health publisher

Kelly Brown

Published by
Chipmunkapublishing
PO Box 6872
Brentwood
Essex CM13 1ZT
United Kingdom

http://www.chipmunkapublishing.com

Copyright © Kelly Brown 2010

Edited by Aleks Lech

Chipmunkapublishing gratefully acknowledge the support of Arts Council England.

Introduction

I was born in London in 1970 and was diagnosed with a mental Illness over ten years ago, and this book tells in fictional form some of the experiences that I had to come to terms with psychologically and just a few of the Spiritual/healing aspects that I've encountered. When I was eighteen, I rather foolishly went to Africa. The trip shocked, disturbed me and made me feel quite unstable. It did however make me into a writer. To balance these feelings of inadequacy and fear, the following summer Wendy and I travelled around Europe, it was a trip full of fun and art. We met many people, but when the trip was nearly over on a train towards nice a man came into our carriage. He was around forty or fifty, and grey, warm and not scary at all. He spoke to us and though he said a lot, and I enjoyed the conversation immensely, when he left I remember only one thing, this was that we should go to the south of France, to the part where France meets Spain into the Mountains. I did go and this very spiritual, wonderful area is where my son's father and his family are from, and it is the most magical amazing place.

'Passages from the Search for Eternal love' began when I started to read biographical books about Picasso. One book in particular, which I haven't seen for years called 'Picasso's women'. I do love Picasso's paintings, particularly his blue period. But more and more I wanted to know how Picasso, like Henry VIII could have loved so many women, loved and been cruel also. Much of my own mental distress has been around the aspect of love, and I have found the in authenticity surrounding love very difficult to understand. One the one hand I like to be open to love, but find that revealing vulnerability just makes some people very cruel and unkind. How does one deal with this without becoming bitter and closed? Well in the end I learnt how to be open to more love, not just to the co-dependant relationship sort that is portrayed by society, but to a universal love, that wasn't about dysfunctional relationships. I found healing in this love; I discovered the spiritual world, angels, guides, and a whole universe of beings and energies that wanted the best for me, for me to shine, and be filled with hope, happiness and joy. The dance in this book relates to the 5rhythums dance practice, which I experienced for a year, which I found an amazing healing practice, and would recommend to anyone who is feeling low, and perhaps lacking in identity. My next book is called "Of the solace between life and death'. Love, peace and happiness.

Passages from the Search for Eternal Love

Eva   I've just finished reading a book about the hedonistic sixties, the decade in which I was conceived, but the decade before I was born, and I am shocked by so much thought of suicide. I look for something underpinning this, perhaps dabbling in drugs that were mind expanding; perhaps the emphasis on youth and beauty, but also perhaps the emphasis on getting to know oneself... an arduous task, a little bit scary.

I dream of subtle truths; I hold a mirror to myself and I know that being Eva is an incarnation, not an absolute truth. I am often drawn of other Eva's. Just now I gaze at a picture of Eva Hesse, a sculptor of dangerous materials. She stands there, knowing herself, liking or perhaps even loving herself, with a peasant scarf on her head, trapping her dark voluminous hair. She is so far away from knowing that she will die very soon. Yet for all my talk of death and suicide, death is not my soft uncomfortable spot, love is. I could cry just having to sound the word 'love'. Mostly they are sharp tears that come quickly and make you gasp. Oddly enough eternal love is different. To meet an eternal love has no emotional ring, for me it is like a quest; almost like I am on a truth-finding mission, to find out all I can about eternal love, and tell it to you. I am not quite ready to finish this quest, hence the passages bit, but I am so glad you are reading it, otherwise this incarnation would feel somehow wasted.

I was on a path, a quite different one- I was an artist. My main goal was to describe reality, a shared reality, of the world of matter and the world of concerns. I went to Hebden bridge on one of my regular trips to stay with my friends there, hang out with their boys, and feel part of a family. I had no partner, and still have no one, mostly because the thoughts that engage me need a lot of space and silence. I hate bickering and blaming, and that's what most couples seem to do, even lovely enlightened couples. But my path changed. I was invited to a workshop run by a very beautiful women called Rosa, and as she uttered the magical words, " learning through love, a chance to find your path and meet your guides," these were the words that I'd waited thirty-five years to hear, and I was ready for them. I don't particularly like residential courses. They remind me of the terrible time I had during my first years at University; as I struggled to get along with people who knew too much about me; what I ate, how I brushed my teeth, how I kept my room, who I had sex with! It was a vulnerable experience, but I knew I wanted to go to Illigruum House, because I had some questions and wanted some answers. I wanted to know what was the point of my life if it had no love. If no-one held me, caressed my being and my cares, told me how beautiful I was, or lived for my growth and happiness.

Also I wanted to talk about my guide. She was a guide, spirit or perhaps just the rumblings of my own mind. But she had just joined me. She often made insightful comments: she was kind, funny and encouraged me. I thought she existed because I spent so much time alone, but recently I was beginning to think she was a guide. She spoke a lot about love, told me often in a joking way. I have really unsuccessful relationships. I seem to meet so many people who I can love, like a nun or mother, but so few that I want to spend much time with. I love to camp outside, to backpack, walk, take local buses, get lost and then find myself part of small communities. I only go to places where I can speak clearly and have regular conversations, so I know France, Spain and Italy well and I always long for a companion. My generation of people like adventure and go to hot cheap countries where you can live for a pound or something. I like drinking lush red wine, eating massive stews of pork and beans, and talking with old people about the members of their families; where they are, what they do, when they are coming back, because generally young people like cities. Young people generally like to be in exciting places, where you make money and spend money, and talk about people you hardly know, but like intensely. I like nature a lot. In nature I come alive.

I hear all the voices of the trees, birds and hills. I travel like one who likes this because I need to, it is the food my soul needs. I find myself again and again, and understand others and the world much better: To step out of the entrenched thinking and my self-pitying wining. To breath good air, rest by trees following their branches, feel the cool breeze and the warm sun. But mostly listen to the whispers of the trees, their wonderful insights gathering in space for the silence to hear...silence to hear.

Eva   The room is grey, the floors are blond wood. We sit together in a circle, with the space to smell each other, but we are strangers. She is bold, upright but not rigid, almost defying age. Her hair is solid white, but so beautifully healthy settling by her chin, curving around her solid black eyes. She is Rosa and she will lead us to the path. It is a path without doubt: A path without forked roads, or sudden Damascus lightening bolts.

Rosa   Two images press together needing to be related. In one my small son leads me through the park, past the loud black crows, whom he mimics, and in the second my Buddhist friend Myomi and me discuss by the kitchen sink the difference between Buddhism and Christianity. "You see", she says, "in Christianity some people want a place for good people and a place for bad people, in Buddhism we realise that we are all sometimes good sometimes bad". But then what she said next hooked into my stomach and never left, "Christ comes as a saviour, very noble, sad, cruel... well in Buddhism we all reincarnate, every single one of us, we all keep coming back again and again, until all, every single one and part of this world are there in the same place...together": I love this, it has hope.

Rosa   One day, a particular sad day, after realising something very cruel about this world I cried and cried a lot. I was so angry about what humans can do, and then I said "why, why are we back here, meaning me and my son." Because I sometimes feel as though I have been back so many times and I feel so much, It's as if I'm 80% Angel and my spirit really has a hard time staying in my body. As young as six I used to levitate and spin above my body. I never told anyone. But now despite everything that is cruel I am happy to be here because I have learnt so much that I didn't know. And I can honestly say despite everything I love this world…eternally, and I feel that it is possible that the world loves us eternally. **How wonderful is that!** But 'what about eternal love?' I hear you say, what about the love that a person can have for another person which they can share eternally, does that exist? Have I known that? I have a story I wish to tell and I guess my seventieth birthday is the best place to start, said Rosa, and we all listened mesmerised.

Love and Vengeance

Eva   I had imagined that we would all be women, that a man, or perhaps the men I knew would not be interested in eternal love, or the stories of an old woman, but we were an even six, and three were men. I felt the way I always did with men, an immediate attraction and pull, which I would have to wrestle with. I always gave my power away to men. But then she started before I had a chance to really tussle with my being.

Rosa From the vessel of verisimilitude emptied of vespers - now her bedroom - once a church hall, she hears noises like the voices of spiders, the whisperings of those no longer alive: Those no longer tangible. We call these ghosts, the un-dead, I call this dark matter because I am a philosopher not a scaremonger. She rented the room because it looked so beautiful from the outside, as so many things and people do, but then inside it became quite different. Dark, Closed, Scary... I shudder just thinking of Alice Bloom, a single woman in her late thirties who feels so alone, that she so messed up her life- that she allowed love to crush her rather than elevate her. The enforced noises irritate her soft sensibility and she wishes to move but doesn't because she lives life passively, allowing life and not herself to make her life-decisions.

The magnitude of all this and more struck Alice Bloom from behind her very busy piled high desk at Norwood library where she worked every day except Wednesdays and Sundays and of course the obligatory four weeks holidays when she felt so depressed. Mostly depression is expected at winter when loneliness seeps into our wounded crevices, but in summer as the busy dash in droves to this paradise or this holiday home the lonely are left at home alone wondering why they live in London in the first place. Vilified with vengeance Alice Bloom, the librarian, sought a way to get back at the man who broke her heart, her life, it was a subtle plan that I now shall tell to you in a way that you might understand.

Rosa   When Alice was eight or nine she had a recurring dream about being on a pirate ship or a slave boat and being the only survivor; everyone else was dead, she looked everywhere but all she could see and smell were the dead and the rotting. Strangely though, and this myself I still don't understand, she fell in love with a blond dead boy. His body was green and blue with death but the blondness of his hair still shone and the subtlety of his being still remained - he was her Love and she endeavoured, whatever, to find on earth, alive, that spirit and marry him. But this longing was lie, a curse planted in her mind by a rather hopelessly sad and lonely ancestor called Lilly.

Rosa   Lilly was from a Romany family and as with many cultures as the eldest daughter her role was to look after her mother until she died, which turned out rather unfortunately to be a very, very long time. Lilly was beautiful with a blast of red fluff for hair, rather pre-Raphaelite. She had many admirers but so powerful was her mother's energy she never defied her imposition and never once even kissed the artist Pablo, whom she adored. And though he begged and begged for the taste of her lips, they embraced but never kissed. So when her mother finally died aged seventy-seven Lilly was already fifty, her blazing hair soft white clouds and her eyes dull and dreary and no one, not even Pablo, ever longed to kiss her lips. So she placed a curse of lovelessness on every single member of the offspring of her brothers and sisters to live forever in unrequited love. Happily for most they allowed love to overcome them but Alice Bloom was less fortunate. She had an image of her eternal love fixed in her mind like a solid stone. She looked for him over and over again until one autumn day she saw what she thought was him. It all began so beautifully, but as you might have guessed ended up sourly, for vengeance only comes with sour endings.

Rosa "What has brought you to me", asked Alice in her soft but curiously passionate voice.
"I love you," he lied.
"How is that possible?" said Alice Bloom, but he didn't answer and although this didn't upset Alice in the slightest, he had found her and that was all that mattered; his matt blonde hair glowed and resonated through her heart. This is the most important question of love, 'how do you love me?' It didn't bother her whether he had been stalking her and it was that kind of platonic, obsessive love, she thought he was what she longed for. He took her hand and they left the library together, already sweethearts. "Your name" she said, insisting on some kind of formality "Vendrimin", he replied without a hint of irony, humour or lie for it was a Friday, a perfect Friday for love.

Passages from the Search for Eternal Love

Rosa Now remember Lilly, Alice Bloom's ancestor? The love of Lilly's life had been the artist we shall call Pablo, for artistic purposes and because he painted like Picasso. Pablo was as dark as a winter's night and just as stormy. He held Lilly close up against an oak tree and begged her for the sweetness of her lips. But she thought there was time enough for love, denied him, denied herself.
"But Pablo, I promised my mother that I would not love anyone until she is dead".

Rosa "You have already broken that promise. I see it in your eyes you are already in love with me". Lilly blushed at the truth as she often did, she felt humiliation at the slightest revealing. Lilly was tempted to place her soft pink lips on his bruised dry ones, it was a moment of time trapped forever in her mind and she died hoping for that kiss, and still cursing, cursing and cursing. When her mother finally died, Lilly was fifty. She was too old for beauty, and too bitter for kindness.
One morning, grey, overcast and restless Alice left the Library, she was the last to leave, and the locking up was her responsibility. She turned the key and slowly turned around and saw again that burnished golden head and sinister smile it; was Vendrimin.
"Where have you been?" She asked obsessively, "You said you would ring, and well I started to think back that maybe you were the kind of guy..."
"That just wants sex, to conquer".
"Yes", said Alice meekly.
"Why would I do that when making love with you was like holding a delicate butterfly in my hand, it was everything..."

"So where do we go from here?" she begged. Vendrimin held Alice's hand firmly and replied "To the circus…High, High we fly…" It was a bitter joke.

Alice became increasingly besotted with Vendrimin, so much so that when after six months and with no warning he dumped her and left her broken hearted she plotted revenge so subtle and cruel, it met vengeance with vengeance.

Rosa   She went to his mother who was in a nursing home in Treviso, began working there, and she told everyone she saw that Vendrimin was the devil, that Isabelle, his mother, had slept with the devil to conceive him. Everyone wanted proof so she whispered in their ear what he had done to her in bed and they all in time believed her. Isabelle who was already ill and tired gave up on life very easily after this, for she believed in part that the soldier who had raped her during the 2nd world war was indeed the devil and her son was no gift from God. She died alone, abandoned and unhappy, cursing the day she gave birth to her son. Curses like these stay, they embitter the energy of the planet.

Vendrimin was the best kisser in the whole of Treviso; he was also the son of a fascist in the village of partisans, and thus a heroic outsider to the girls of the village and some one to be mistrusted by the boys. When he was twelve, the girls in the school playground would queue just for one kiss. So when Alice Bloom became just another kiss, and another pathetic attempt at intimacy for poor Vendrimin, he thought only of conquest. This kiss however, for her it was so special that it lit her from the inside so brightly she became like a human lamp. For him it was nothing greater or less than the first or the last. The un-reciprocity of life is one of its largest pitfalls; for one everything, for the other the same, the same....

Rosa By the time he was thirty-seven Vendrimin had read everything worth reading in the philosophy section, he had skimmed all the large and small art books at West Norwood library and it was with fatigue and a kind of boredom that he approached Alice Bloom's desk. He wore a tight orange t-shirt and some purposely badly fitted jeans that settled on his eloquent hips. Alice Bloom wore a half circle green skirt and brown blouse, he wondered only for a second why she was dressed as a tree. He then passed on to think about would be to kiss those dry brittle lips, and moisten them. Alice on the other hand looked at Vendrimin and realised that a fashionably dressed educated man like that would never consider her in all her dullness. But still she wondered what it would be like to wake up every night and day next to that blond shiny hair and broad mouth and shoulders. As it was their intensity was miss-matched very early on. True love for her, another inconsequential conquest for him.

Rosa The death of his mother affected Vendrimin more than he had expected even though he didn't love or believe in love. But the story about him being the son of the devil spun around Trevisio and the surrounding Venetian area like a bad smell and he hated the whisperings that followed him wherever he went.

But that was not yet true vindication for that Alice Bloom. She wanted to arrange for the heart breaker to have his heart broken. This was difficult but not impossible. In much the same way that Lilly vindicated Pablo for that promised kiss, in lingering love; when Pablo indicated that Lilly was too old for his love at fifty, or thereabouts, Lilly paid the most beautiful muse like girl, a philosophy student and life model, to seduce Pablo beyond his own reason, so that he would lose all sense. Pablo fell for Rosa like a fish for a hook, and Rosa was vindictive, vixen-like, with a vulture's passion. Pablo begged for her marriage but she never even kissed him, not once, not ever. Lilly paid her to break Pablo, after all a man should never promise love to a gipsy woman and then renege.

Passages from the Search for Eternal Love

Childhood and Kierkegaard

Eva   We three women slept in one room. Elena apologised, saying that she was a noisy sleeper, and I grimaced because I often find the passage between states difficult to find. But despite this I slept soundly. It might have been the camomile tea and lavender oil burner, both new to my way of thinking. I had dreams in dreams that seemed to be their own reality; dreams that showed me that I was on a journey, and perhaps a little more awake than I had been, although I had no logical ideas for how the stories of an old woman could do this, as she seemed no more enlightened than me. The breakfast was a noisy affair. The whole of Illigruum house were together, and the children who I hadn't heard last night were so loud I felt myself becoming irritable. Sensing this about my mood I took my porridge, banana and green tea outside and found a suitable warm spot by a tree. My mind turned on you as it often does and I wondered which philosophy, which religion, would give me the grace to walk the path that would create our togetherness. I had already opted for patience, to wait in a rather conscious way to know you, and in knowing you, love you and be loved, this had worked with friendship, and you it seemed would be my greatest friend, my desired friend.

Rosa   I was brought up by my father Andrew, in an area between St Ives and Zennor, in Cornwall, where we lived in a cluster of small old cottages with our friends who were also artists. My beautiful father loved women and I was the product of something that was sexual rather than romantic. It was a brief affair with a girl whom my father described as 'rather rude and brutal'. She found it hard to love me, because I reminded her of my father, whereas he had loved me from the very first moment when I looked like an alcoholic baby seal, all red-faced with dark oily hair.

Luckily for me my father was kind, thoughtful and always available. He was a painter and he didn't find the two enterprises, painting and nurturing, incompatible, due to his good nature and natural gift. I know of many artists who struggle with their gift, leaving them with little time for anything other than art. Although now a health visitor would have had concerns about the toxicity of the paint next to my crib, or high-chair, most health professionals praised my father for not putting me in a home. He was charming in a gentle way and gorgeous, lit brightly from inside, with golden eyes.

His paintings were everywhere. I loved them because they had people in them and they told stories. Many of his friends just painted in shapes and colours, and I thought this inferior. The cottage was very untidy and we were very poor, as he sold very little. I didn't notice our poverty when I was small. I knew few children, only the other painters, who dressed the same in faded canvas trousers and shirts, and who ate very simply, drinking wine most evenings. But when my aunt came on the scene and I went to school I noticed all our inadequacies, particularly that we didn't have sheets, or much crockery, and that we were very thin and a little dirty. But looking back now it was the best of times, full of intensity and happiness, and I am so glad of my

Passages from the Search for Eternal Love

father's creativity for inspiring me to go to University. I didn't want to be a painter though, I felt too shy for all the socialising that seems to go with painting. I wanted to be a philosopher and writer and was inspired by Kierkegaard, not just because of my very handsome professor Jonathan, but by the idea that we can philosophise through stories as opposed to logic.

The Seduction of Books

Rosa   Fifty is rarely the age of a woman's prime. Usually there is too much yearning for the youth that's gone. I am seventy-something, and so passed thinking about youth that I believe I am becoming radiant again. I was inspired in this area by Barbara Hepworth, who became more and more beautiful the older she got. Her house in St Ives is more garden than house, more studio than home, but unlike some artists who give everything in a kind desperation to attain something beyond humanity, Barbara seemed rather balanced.

I remember the day I met her; she was so elegant in a French beret, and loose pocketed jeans. Her skin patchy, as happens with sun and age, looked also soft, revealing elegant bones. Strangely, I would never have been the philosopher I am if it wasn't for those impossible questions about space and time that her sculpture posed. How long a life: How short a life. I am now the age that Barbara was before she died, and although I always expected to get here, always imagined myself old, it seems today that I am here for one purpose, and one purpose alone: The unfolding of stories of love. Love stories; epic, grand, small, fleeting…

I have never liked many books. Some books linger in the mind. Sometimes you find your mind all cluttered up with so many dusty corners. Some books don't leave. Some books, well you can't understand them straight away, they are there waiting for the right moment in time, events, situations and reflections come and go. These books take up more space than the space on a shelf. So when Kierkegaard asks the question 'what is it that makes our life not despair?' I understand that it is love, love and love again.

Rosa   Some people live through books. Others fall in love with characters from books. Alice Bloom fell in love with Prince Charming, obvious but true. Most girls fall in love with the dresses from the books, purple, golden and silver, bustling, bold and feminine. Alice Bloom fell and fell and fell for Prince Charming, and she looked for him everywhere. That Friday all bitter and grey, she glimpsed above her book about flying and dancing and saw his feathery blond head emerge from a red jumper, his cheeks boldly red, almost as if tinged by make-up or from running flat out, or perhaps kissing passionately against an alley wall - there he was. Alice Bloom studied every second. First the colour of his eyes: Looking and looking, to get the right shade - grey. Then his gestures, the way he turned each page, eager and curious. How he studied and studied his book, a book about the great masters of painting. How he seemed stuck on Goya and then he flicked to Poussin. He had to be a painter - but as we know painters are never Prince Charming, they never marry, never rescue, they change from muse to muse at will. She remembered her aunt Lilly and how Pablo the painter had torn her heart apart; how cruelly she cried, and cried. How could he be a painter and her Prince Charming? It wasn't possible.

Rosa   Alice Bloom vowed to ignore him but as he stood

there at her desk mixing his fantasy with her possibility she found against all will that she simply said yes to everything he asked. Yes, she liked working in the library, yes she was free on Thursdays, yes she would like to meet him for a drink despite him already having a girlfriend and him letting her know this.

Rosa   For most people love is not eternal; they do not expect to find their eternal love, and just stay with the first person that interests them, or is kind, who grabs them and holds them tight as though it would be so easy. That's why the marriage vows are like an abstract thorn in the foot, no one every really promises those words, they just say them because that's what is required. Yet we all know that authenticity doesn't come from repeating something verbatim, but rather from what we say spontaneously and freely. Pablo had said a lot of things that seemed to Lilly to be said authentically and they were; at twenty Pablo was a poor and passionate man at arts school: A student who decided to paint when the art world was giving up on paint in favour of space and sculpture. He saw Lilly Hutton one day when she was shopping for groceries, and he was sketching with his mind. He noticed the contrast of the greens falling out of her basket and her hair falling out of her hairpins. Her hair was red like an autumn apple, a curly frizzy halo that framed her hopeful face.

Rosa   Even if Pablo never kissed her the promise of Pablo's kiss resonated on Lilly's lips a thousand times. It didn't however resonate with her that in her twenties his love had been ardent, while in her thirties it was friendly, and by forty it was absent. Pablo always seemed to be with a version of Lilly, and that version always stayed in her late twenties, but it was never Lilly. Pablo didn't need Lilly to continue to be his muse because a version of Lilly existed everywhere, the corners of bookshops, alone at bars or at gallery openings. Meanwhile boredom was stealing away Lilly's life as her life became impossibly hard, as her mother became older and more infirm. Yet Pablo bringing her flowers regularly was for Lilly a continuation of his promised love. Pablo brought daffodils in March, cornflowers in September, and October's blues in October.

Rosa   By the time of her mother's funeral, Pablo brought an amazing array of white lillies, he was moderately rich through painting, and Lilly took this as a sign that their love could at last begin. But for Pablo there was no beginning, only an ending. Pablo wasn't cruel to bring Margarita to the Funeral; he knew no better way than to make it obvious to Lilly that she was now too old for his love. Margarita was obviously an artist too, she was dressed in a simple outfit of black leggings and jumper, her hair in a simple ponytail as was fashionable at the time made Lilly so angry she could feel the heat in her tears behind her eyes. She followed her mind through the funeral, to the wake, to a few days for solace, right to the day that she intended to march to Pablo's house and challenge him and his promise of eternal love and then realised that there were no words for that conversation, only a hopeless look. Pablo thought immediately of the first day he had seen Lilly and how ardent he had been, of how bright she had been. By comparison she looked like a piece of tarnished jewellery, she could never be as she was and as she was Pablo wasn't interested. I guess the best revenge would be for Lily to suddenly become radiant, the most beautiful jewel, but this isn't a fairy tale and we know by now that most plastic surgery just makes people look rather odd. For Pablo to see Lilly as beautiful, Lilly would first have to be beautiful for herself, and like I said few women are beautiful at fifty, too much nostalgia, too much lost youth and in Lilly's case too much anger. And Pablo needed perhaps to see the world a bit more spiritually, and less about his palette of intention.

Rosa   Alice wasn't angry, she was that emotion beyond anger wherein we often use words like livid, enraged, incensed. Through her parentage of Irish gypsy and black Caribbean she came across a magic so powerful that it was able to change the pattern of time, to sacrifice linear time and a largely uneventful life, without mystery or difference she became known to herself as the witch inside. The book that inspired this transformation was a book on the history of the Caribbean. A black book, medium sized and hard backed that she found on a brief trip to Zambia, and a belief that it was worth talking to the voices in your head - because they may just be your ancestors. So she spun a spell of unrequited love on Venerating and it stuck. Oh yes, the powerful energy of witches is necessary to balance out the unchecked egos of men.

Eva   The room went quiet, as we three women looked at the men to check their expressions. Over centuries, and centuries of killing us and calling us witches, suddenly it was OK to be a witch - here and now in this place of safety. I knew very little about it - just the distinction between dark magic and light. Light magic was anything one did for oneself and dark was anything one did for someone else, even making someone fall in love with you, as opposed to letting them fall of their own free will. In the quietness my mind roved and as the others left to start the evening rituals I was left thinking about magic.

I remembered something that happened in New York. I was sitting in a bohemian bar watching a beautiful poetess seduce my artist boyfriend, when an old man, realizing that my boyfriend wasn't paying me any notice, came over. We chatted for a while about dance, and other things, he was really old but he began dancing, and I wasn't sure if he was being humorous but his face looked really serious. Then he began massaging my back. Not in a warm friendly way, but cold and hard, but I couldn't move, or say stop...I told the story to Rosa as I passed her and she told me this...

Rosa He was a shaman, and whether you believe in this kind of thing or not is inconsequential, it exists. It's not faith that makes a shaman able to shift your assemblage point so that you see reality ever so slightly differently. I bet the world was never the same again. Like Alice in Wonderland or something similar. It's very difficult to find the language to explain but reality is not a hard, cold surface, it is a multi-myriad, multi-faceted, multi-possible reality that exist and once you are aware of this in a very real, tangible way, once you know this many things are possible.

Passages from the Search for Eternal Love

The paradox of eternal love

Eva   It took me so long to get here, so much crying - trying to understand. But that night I dreamt the understanding. A man far away is my love. I recognise him as my eternal love, and he recognises me in the same way. Yet each step he takes towards me represents a passage of time. I try to keep him in view but he changes so fast, morphing into different people - different hair, different face, and different character. Until finally he reaches me: We are together at last, but the person he looks like is not the same person I saw from far away, and I no longer love him.

Rosa   When I reflect about time passing I fall upon its spin of layered experience - this we'll call existence. Once we knew nothing and pressed only to know more. Now we know a lot and press backwards as though there could be undoing. We only really got here because along the way we realised that there are certain tasks, and it is only known here in this room with you feeling the weight of not just our lives, but the lives of our ancestors, that I believe we have come to see that our greatest task is trying to understand eternal love, in all its manifestations.

By this I mean everything from movies with their hard and fast certainty to death. There is beauty in being able to fall in love with heroes whose actions and movements never change: To everything about love and spirituality. Does this universe love us truly and deeply? I have collected these stories as representatives of existence, as representatives of that which has brought me closer to understanding that first there is a question- perhaps dignified and small and almost imperceptible, a kind of silence, which asks 'how can we be present in our life enough to make our lives an understanding of love?'

Eva   When I met Rosa at Illigruum house, the commune in West Yorkshire where the course " learning through love", was held, I was impressed very early on how uniquely authentic her speech was. I was curious to know these stories she referred. Illigruum house was the kind of community that I'd always longed to live in but could never find. It didn't exist on the internet, and no matter how longingly I thought about it the pathway towards it never appeared.

Rosa   Me, if I had been so lucky I would have been a nun: A nun with such fantastic faith that my one life would change the path of a universe. We would all move from this dark cavernous and sad untruth to something so bright and hopeful that there would be no place for suicide. To not be here right now in the beautiful powerful moment would beyond all credulity. And there I am talking as if I am that nun when my life is so far from nun like.

There is another parallel universe in which I am on a mission, and it's such a long one. So long and so deep that I've actually forgotten who I am, in the first place. Thank God for love, because without this caring, loosing, hoping quest we all could be on deep deep missions forgetting who we are.

Eva   Rosa took a deep breath before she engaged in the next passage knowing as she did that perhaps that some of us on the course were Christians.

Rosa I blame the story of Noah's arc for allowing us to dwell on the concept of a journey a boat- of being together with our loved one, two by two. So there we are constant with tales of flooding, with experiences of flooding. It floods it floods, but who is our other? Who would go with us, or run to be with us, and where is the boat that will finally rescue us?

There was a boat once, many huge boats and many people. One of my ancestors, who I will call Kyra, was on that boat, though I know not where she was, only where she was going to. She was going to slavery. We all have seen the pictures of those slaves ships, the conditions, cattled humans. This ship became sick, rapidly everyone was struck by a devastating illness, we might call it cholera, and Kyra remained somehow immune. Perhaps her ancestry had already experienced slavery and had developed a hardiness- we know not. All we know is the Kyra lived on that boat hoping to get close enough to land to swim to safety. But the waters were long and open and her experience prolonged and she became accustomed to the look of death and illness, of the state of human decomposition, its colour and smell, and she knew no fear. Strange though it may seem, the absence of what we call life enabled a whole new dimension of life and eventually love.

One night she slept in a corner of the ship that she had cleared and made homely. She cried as usual, feeling so alone and so without hope, but eventually she slept and felt the comfort of sleeping, of being known and understood in a world that made no sense, and as she drifted awake she felt the actual presence of warm embracing arms, and a voice where there should have been silence. She cried, relief? Happiness? Now whether Kyra had a ghost lover, or friend, Spirit, or God she had all the presence she needed to get through what seems to be the most difficult of all journeys. It strikes me that perhaps this is what is meant by the suffering of Christ, perhaps his suffering, so great as it was, will mean we will always have a presence there in our greatest need, when we are really suffering. That's really beautiful. Christ is there during our most difficult of all journeys as an embodiment of eternal love. I wish in many ways that I had had a ghost lover, because my search for eternal love has sent me on too many quests, through to many hearts, understanding too many hearts. I really should have been a nun.

Eva   We all laughed at the idea of this seductive old woman, whose eyes twinkled when she talked about love, knowing really that she wouldn't have missed her life for the world, and moved towards the kitchen for our warming calming drinks. Afterwards we again made our way to our dormitories and the sweet smell of lavender and incense, and though I felt comfortable and warm in that cosy bed, in that cosy room, I couldn't help wishing that I had a pair of warm real arms wrapped around me and wondered how many people felt the same way?

But that night I again had that powerful nightmare. The dream said it all. In the distance is my eternal love - whom I know at a glance. As he moves towards me each step is a passage of time, he changes, shifts almost imperceptibly, his hair, his face, his smile, his look, his intelligence, all shifting away from that which I knew in an instance. Until he is standing in front of me: There to be known, and I have to concede that he is the same soul and although we have travelled through space and time together and although I know that he is still my eternal love, I do not love this man. I feel so sad, so alone.

Eva   To love easily from far away and not close: So easy the seduction and the less that is known the easier it seems. I have experienced so many knowing glances, and you made sense of it saying perhaps that we were just seeing God for a moment. But it is your glance, which is the best of all. From the day when we danced, and I with back turned, glimpsed you over my shoulder, and gave you a glance so easily misread, which you captured and gave back. To put into words it was the mirror of my glance. I took it home and kept it in my mind like a butterfly. The thought that you are mine to love, the idea scares me shitless. Could it be you who could know me at the end and the beginning of time; who would love regardless and still love? That someone who knows so little, not much more than a glance should love us for eternity? And as Rosa's stories reverberates, I find a new ending.

"What has brought you to me?", asked Alice in her soft but curiously passionate voice.

"I've been watching and following you for several

days, your routine, so precise just like you hair, so perfect. I love those thirties twists you wear. The way you bundle your black-red hair on top just as women in the thirties used to".

And though there was something slightly odd about his manner it mattered not to Alice, he had found her and that was all that was of concern. His matt blond hair glowed and resonated through her heart. It didn't bother her in the slightest what kind of 'love' it was, and that it had neither much care nor concern. He grabs her hand with a force she felt she needed, when actually all she needed was gentleness.

Alice became increasingly besotted with Vendrimin, so when after six months and with no warning he dumped her and left her broken hearted she plotted a revenge so subtle, so still, that the truth of it still exists inexpressibly. The un-reciprocity of life is one of its largest pitfalls; for one everything, for the other the same, the same…

She whispered " please look no more, please look no more, for I am here…" but all ready he was running, fast and high, his mind flipping images, and she has to be brave. She moved to Finland, to the north where the Sámi live. Rode horses, swam in cold beautiful lakes, spoke to whispering trees, walked with silver furred wild dogs and eventually fell in love with Soren. Dark blond with rough weathered skin, he reciprocated until his death a quiet almost sombre love, until he died at seventy-four of nothing in particular.

Eva   My friends who were to experience arranged marriages, were told by their mothers that it was possible to fall in love with anyone. But how could that be possible with our attractions being so different, so related to us? I went through a stage of loving wild, imaginative men, the kind who would never ask me to marry them, who would never be clear about who I was to their friends, and I loved the freedom of this. But now I hate this kind of man; I hate his cigarettes, his smell of too much booze, his cold-hearted distance, his roll call of women. Now I'm again like a teenager who loves easily, and likes very beautiful attractive people.

People with shiny clean hair, and clean teeth, flat controlled tummies, and beautiful well kept feet. Who speak easily of love, of God, who are kind and have faith. I have no more time for narcissistic, ugly boozy men who are unkind and rough and want to be rock-stars or famous artists, who suffer unnecessarily and would make me suffer unnecessarily too. I had only just discovered this about myself, and I didn't feel guilty about it, just relieved of this difficult path that I had been on.

Eva   My guide helped me hear myself. I wasn't afraid of her presence, or non-presence, I'd had other guides before but she was the first guide who made sense, and who made me laugh with her funny insights about me and the world. Through my heart-break she reminded me how special I was, but it was only now hearing the different stories that I realised how many Vendrimins and Pablos I had met, cruel unkind men who twisted and controlled, creating upset on upset.

Unravelling my concept of beauty

Eva You said that it was beautiful, the idea that death was on our shoulder, that we had to leave constantly with impermanence, and I gasped, not quite believing that you would find that beautiful. Perhaps this is why I love you the most, because you are not what you seem, and discovering you delights me.

It had always stayed with me, the notion that Buddha found enlightenment by resting by a tree, and long before I believed in fairies, ghosts or white witches I believed in trees and their whisperings. I took my lunch of home made hummus and salad and nestled next to a beautiful old tree, to feel the breeze, to be close to happiness, and found before too long that I had a companion, David. He had the face of a farmer, whatever that may mean, and soft, friendly eyes, that had none of the intelligence of his voice. I was annoyed at first to have my space interrupted, but gradually I became enraptured by our conversation on beauty.

Eva "I am again like a child", he said, "all the things I have know are no longer rock, stone, or even sand, they are like the sound of the wind blowing though the trees'. Not quite understanding what he meant I encouraged him to explain further. "Take beauty", he said, "I had never realised that before now. I didn't realise how beautiful an expressive face can be. That a warm, open and kind expression could make beautiful a face - I think I am falling in love with Rosa... oh I do not want to marry her, or own her. I am just surprised by how beautiful I find her, and this of course reveals perhaps that I had a misconceived concept of beauty. I have perhaps come to value her expressions even more than the words of her story". I nodded in agreement, and turned my gaze to his face and found that he too looked beautiful, under the tree, with his warmth, understanding and love of an old woman. I realised to that I could enjoy the beauty of his face without wanting to own it, that the moment was enough. We inhabited a silence and in this silence I realised that I too had a misconception of beauty. Perhaps we are encouraged to see beauty and take steps to flirt, desire, plan our futures around a moment of radiance, which may not be about that person at all but that moment, and you can't marry a moment, hence so much disappointment.

Rosa It was inevitable that I would too want to be an artist. I left Cornwall, and went to Wimbledon, for no obvious reason. I went there to study Art, finding it relatively easy to get in- I had very strong talent at drawing. But pretty soon it became obvious that art school was nothing about ability, and everything about ideas and concepts. One had to dress with identity, listen to the right music, and form a kind of gang of sorts. Growing up surrounded by adults gave me a lot of intensity and authenticity and I found my fellow students vacuous and they seemed to find me too intense. Also despite my talents in drawing I was pushed towards sculpture, which unlike in the early twentieth century, when Modigliani wanted to be a sculptor but found it too expensive, sculpture was now for the masses, and anything could be made out of anything. I hated these so called sculptures, I found them grotesque; they lacked beauty. So when pushed to sculpt, I turned away from art and found myself attending the Philosophy lectures. Philosophy made sense to me, by helping me to find a language to describe my new outsider-ness. I gave up art and moved to the North, which was relatively cheap to be a student in. I moved to Heptonstall, Hebden Bridge, a small village where Sylvia Plath is buried, that is pretty, remote, and built in stone, and I rented a large decaying cottage.

Rosa　When I reflect about time passing I fall upon its spin of layered experience - this we will call existence. Once we knew nothing and pressed only to know more. Now we know a lot and press backwards as though there could be undoing. We only really got here because along the way we realised that there are certain tasks, and it is only here alone in this cold room feeling the wait of ten thousand years ago that I come to know that one of my greatest tasks is to answer the question of 'eternal love'.

Rosa　James' eyes were a pale soft green, seeming kind beyond belief, too kind, like a gentle animal. They were the colour of the murky waters of Venice; With an intensity of meaning. How in the lived life we get to know and understand the changing face and those eyes once fresh are dulled by life, jumping alive, rarely if ever singing. I never got to see all the ways that time would change James eyes. Mostly, as with all love, he existed as a moment, a kind and warm moment.

I have seen love transform, and have been

transformed by it and my mind settles on the worst. The worst case I can think of was Jacqueline: The most beautiful woman of my father's generation, with her beautiful long brown hair and pearly-almond eyes. At her wedding her suitors lined up in a trailing path to give her a farewel kiss; All handsome, cheeky and promising. Her husband to be however was none of the above. At although I was only eight at the time, I knew he was sullen, rude and aggressive.

After the wedding we didn't see Jacqueline for several years, until eventually we saw her bare cold un-comely apartment and her appearance so transformed by unhappiness and un-loving anger. She was huge, enormous and sofa-like, her sad hair frizzled and decaying. I sat with my father listening to how love can transform one so. Her words revealed nothing but boredom, yet her eyes revealed everything. I saw a mind spin on a pivotal moment, it played in my mind as it had in her's; of a time when she sailed along her adoring suitors and landed with Mr Grumpy, but I couldn't ask why. My father's other friend Louise furnished the truth, 'we rarely marry the person we love, we marry the person who comes along after the person we love has sailed away'.

Eva   I am surprised how the world shifts one way and then the other. It's a few years since the beginning of my Shamanic training with Rosa, but I remember when Rosa introduced her readings she asked us to meditate on our sameness.

I tried to meditate on my sameness, feeling only

my difference, and it worked for a while. Until the cruellest of twists opened a cavernous space between reality and non-reality and I was again forced to acknowledge, to face the fact that I am so different. That only allowing my mind this wordless sentence, makes me cry. I am so different, that I will always exist alone and unknown, with no one to know my depth. Last year I thought that the behaviour of people in winter really scared me, this year it is the non-behaviour. The seeming normality of the others who see the thread of my existence, that scares me to the sharpest depth, beyond flesh to bone. Winter is the season that really asks you to go deeper, and I have to, why don't they, how can they be so bland without fear on fear, as the parks and gardens die and the day is more moon, and night, starkly bright sun and ashen light.

My life has adapted and the question of being, wrapped around it, tangled and sharp, can I find meaning? I would like to be a smart bear, warm and half-alive in my hibernation dwelling; instead I am a lone wolf, beautiful disturbed. You once said, 'Eva, no-one can see your thoughts', perhaps that was true when I was simple and young. But my layered years, nothing forgotten, weighed each word, each expression, with difference. I found myself shouting, "I am not like you". "OH GOD I AM NOT LIKE YOU ALL."

Eva   We were all surprised by my outburst but Rosa's face crumbled in recognition, she seemed so white haired and serene. But there she stood in the valley of sameness.

Rosa You know James said 'The love that lasts the longest is the love that is never returned'. It filled me with the greatest sadness that he believed this, even as I loved him, even before I knew exactly what it meant. Love was so many journeys.

The questions of being, the questions of love

Eva   Here there was enough silence and space for me to hear the rumblings inside my head, and as ashamed as I felt, the fact that I had so much potential for love but that I was not in a great relationship upset every fabric of my being. I worried also that I was becoming so used to silence, so used to my routine of aloneness that I would never again be open enough to share my being with another. Holding on to my gratitude rather than my shame I found myself sharing time with Hadley, one of the three men from the course. Hadley had met his wife at University. He was a beautiful man with chestnut, chin length hair, warm brown eyes and knowledge of femininity. I asked him what he felt, having spent nearly twenty years in a relationship. He said that he felt a co-dependence, and a need to create space. He went on to say that he felt that he would have grown more, experienced more, definitely travelled more and had more friends if he had been single. But when I told him I hadn't had a relationship since everything had fallen through with Paul, a long time ago, he looked sorry for me.

Rosa   The kind of poverty I lived; a bohemian squalor. It may have looked attractive from the outside, but living it made me feel an outsider, an ashamed outsider, and followed me through my early adult life. I left Cornwall and my dad to go to Wimbledon art school, it was London, but it was South-west and allowed me to feel able to get home if something happened, even if it was a long train journey. I was accepted on the drawing degree, and loved every minute of my classes, and the generous feedback from tutors. But when the classes were finished I didn't know what to do with myself. I was rarely invited anywhere and struggled to make lasting friendships with the other students who listened to a lot of music, drank a lot, had sex and fun. I had no idea now to have fun and alcohol made me very ill. It took me the best part of a year to realise that the others wore bohemianism- to them it was a dress-code, not a way of life, and when term came to an end they went back to the safe and comfortable middle-class lives in the Cotswolds, Sussex, Surrey or the like.

Going home to Andrew, with a deep smell of dirt and paint, meant more squalor, and more poverty as Andrew had given up teaching and lived only from his paintings. I usually had more money than him, and as my grant wasn't much, this made me really sad and depressed. He was often so immersed in his painting that he had little time for anything domestic, and even conversations about my drawing were an unwanted distraction. Emotionally I needed a home. So I moved up north and rented a large cottage, making a home of my own. It was a beautiful yellow cottage in the hills of Yorkshire, in the village of Heptonstall, close to Hebden Bridge. The textile industry had collapsed and no one wanted to live there, so I rented it for practically nothing. I also bought myself an old car so that I could get to and from University in Leeds, where I had enrolled on a course of European Philosophy and Literature. I loved the course; it focused on the questions of being, or Ontology, and I immersed myself in thoughts and ideas about the questions of being; who am I? How do I feel? How do you feel? Is there a God? Is there a soul? I loved every minute of it. At last I felt that I had my place in the world. Also I had my own home so didn't feel the need to go back to Andrew, but we corresponded by letters, and I like this much better as Andrew was able to say in writing what he could not say out loud, and as each day passed I felt more whole, as I learnt how to keep my home clean and pretty. All I needed were some friends, and I was becoming someone interesting to befriend.

Eva   We ate our vegetarian supper together in silence, amongst the others at Illigruum house who were there, adults and children, although we had our own table that we on Rosa's course gravitated to. I wanted to be closer to Hadley, and as Rosa finished this part of her story, I wasn't sure why, but after lunch I asked him whether he would like to come for a walk after dinner. He looked a bit worried, but then his face softened, as if acknowledging that he was safe with me. I enjoyed watching Hadley as he ate, and his expression that seemed to hold a question, and when we walked in the evening light I held his arm, in a warm but friendly way, as I needed to ask him something. I asked him if he had stayed with his partner because he wanted to, or because it was easy. He looked at me as if I had asked him something rude so I explained that I had only met one person that I felt I had loved, and it had not been reciprocated, so I wanted to know if I had been unlucky, or whether the love issue was much easier for other people. He told me that his wife was a very kind and giving person and this made her very lovable, that he didn't hunger for passion, or excitement, and perhaps this was my problem. I agreed, for me passion and love were synonymous and I would never compromise on this, that love had to be a visceral deeply connected vibration, but that I didn't see this as a problem. He then asked me if I believed in eternal love, the kind of love that spans eternity through space and time, and if so how important would passion be. I said yes I did believe in eternal love, and that as far as I was concerned passion would be the glue. He then asked me to consider whether I knew the difference between lust and passion, and as we walked in the dark, close and familiar, I realised that perhaps I didn't know a difference, or how one could tell one from the other.

It was an emotional night, a painful awakening, But I realised that if I did believe in eternal love, and if I did have an eternal love in which I had no way of recognising that person but attraction, passion or possibly lust, that that really wasn't good enough. I realised I was not accepting the stillness in my life as an opportunity to become aware of myself, and what I truly wanted. That I was always lurching from crises to crises and gave no space, to hope, wish, pray. I cried a lot in my sleep and found a hard cold space where my anger existed. It stood between me and love; as a block, or a door, or a gateway, and I had to find out. This anger was like a vixen attacking me and destroying my hope, so that I didn't even now what my hopes were.

The steps towards love

Rosa   The cottage was already called Illigruum house went I arrived. I had no idea what it meant, but I wanted to change it's name to well-igruum house because the yellow cottage gave me the confidence with which to bloom and flourish. I did well at university, and found that not having friends or a relationship gave me ample time to read and reflect, and I easily gained a First. But my studying carried on as I had so much I wanted to research. I enjoyed my weekends too, and went for long walks in the hills, made lovely food from the cheap fruit and vegetables from the market, and after dinner would watch the sky from my garden, its signs and clues often teasing me.

The cottage was two cottages knocked into one, and had too many rooms for just me but I didn't want to spoil this comfortable space, financially there was no need as the owner rented it to me so cheaply, having no need for a remote cottage in the humid hills of West Yorkshire.

Rosa   I felt that I was giving myself a well-needed period of recovery, and felt quite happy in my aloneness, and this must have shown as I found myself, for the first time, making some good friends. Not the sort who were looking for friends with kudos, or had an agenda, but really lovely genuine people, the sort of people that I had always wanted to know. In my journey from Heptonstall to Leeds, at first I never noticed anyone but the sky, but I often saw Rufus and Rebecca, and their beautiful blond healthy boys on my way to get some milk at the post office. They always seemed to be outside, talking to a neighbour or watching the boys play. Rufus was a very kind psychologist, whose work was very radical. He insisted that mental illness was a very real and useful response to an ill society and insane family behaviour. His partner Rebecca was one of the most beautiful women I have ever met. She had a glow about her of love and happiness, she was always warm towards me and I loved it. They sometimes passed by on their walks and I would give the boys milk and fruitcakes, and we three would drink tea and gaze into the wood fires that I made only on occasions.

Rosa   Most books on love I've read always say the same thing, that you have to be complete on your own before you can know whether the other person added to you existence, whether your life was better with them than without them. In many ways the silence and stillness I endured at home gave me a head start in this direction, and in most people's company I looked forward to being alone on my own. One night it was Halloween, a big event in Hepstonstall where adults and children dressed up, playing at being ghouls, spirits and witches.

That Halloween I was prepared with sweets and money for the boys. I opened the door to a crowd of adults and children bubbling with fun, and Rufus invited me to the after party of real music and a bonfire. I also met Issy and Allan, a lovely liberal Jewish couple, who had an open relationship, which surprisingly seemed to work. Issy had very frizzy very grey long hair and a cold no-nonsense face and Allan had a very friendly gaze that made you feel really special. They had two girls around the same age as Rufus's boy and they played well together. There was also Sarah, a social worker who was pregnant, and seemed more efficient than kind, and her partner Peter who was a hippy who used to be in the armed forces. And then there was James. He was Rufus' brother, but I had never met him and I found myself drawn to him in a way that was so strong and connected that I wanted to be close to him; to sit by him, place my head on his knee, his hand in my hand. He wasn't light and kind like Rufus, he was dark and closed, wolfish and sombre, but when he played the guitar and sang, his whole being lit up like an angel, and I felt so attracted to him - and as the light of the fire warmed his gaze I saw that his green eyes were not dark and moody, they were light and playful, the warmest green I had ever seen.

Rosa   "What do you do?" I asked when he finished playing.
"I make and repair, and play stringed instruments, everything from the harp to the fiddle. I may be the only male harp player in the country," he jested.
Silence and reciprocation happened for a while as we looked at each other as though our being was a map of our soul.
"And you...?"
"I think a lot," I mumbled embarrassed.
"And that's an occupation!" he laughed again teasing me, making me feel special.
"It is if you write about those thoughts...in an interesting way, and that's what I try to do" I said,

regaining my reality.

Rosa   That was enough for a first conversation. It was a step into a knowing and a wanting to be known. My eyes spend the rest of the evening watching his face, trying to make a perfect record of his face, which I would try to recall when I was on my own. Later I found out that he too had studied art as a younger man but had turned away from it, for similar reasons to me, and between talking about art and being, we had so much to talk about, and when we didn't talk we enjoyed just looking at each other.

Eva   After hearing Rosa's story, and with my walk with Hadley in my mind I started to think that maybe I needed to change my internal thinking. This thinking that had shaped my existence, but was not necessarily an intrinsic part of my being, although I held on so strongly. I thought about Paul and realised that he wasn't kind. Yet if I were asked which quality I would expect my eternal love to possess kindness would be the main one. How was it possible to live such a contradiction? I lit a candle and made my first attempt at prayer. Not a prayer in crises, because I couldn't cope - but a prayer from stillness, from listening to myself, a prayer of kindness to myself. I asked to be in a kind, loving relationship, with a kind person who would love me for who I was, with whom I could grow and develop, be myself and be happy. And I gave it no time scale, so there would be no anxiety about when. I was no longer lurching from tragedy to tragedy but existing in a still point, and this still point felt calm, quiet, happy, and wonderful.

Why do we bother with love?

Eva   "Why do we bother with love?" I asked Rosa. "None of the greatest love stories make for happiness".

Rosa   "Yes, you're right", she mused. "One of the saddest I can recall was Eleanor Carrington, who spent six dramatic years with Max Ernst, experiencing the wildest passion, when they met as painters.

They left Paris to hide from the Nazis, hiding with passion in the South of France, living on painting love and desire. Then Ernst left because his he was Jewish and feared the camps and Eleanor went crazy and just avoided incarceration in a mental asylum, by cunning and connections, and marriage. When interviewed at seventy she snapped at the interviewer. "Why does everyone focus on this part of my life, it was only six god-dam years?" Well that's the truth, the greatest love affair of your life maybe three months, six months or six god-dam years. We live so much longer, with ourselves, alone with ourselves, either wishing to be together or wishing to be free." A tear fell freely from Rosa's eye and she made no attempt to stop it, though I didn't know whom she cried for, but I hugged her clumsily and she continued.

"Once I was watching television, and two famous people, musicians who became a couple walked along a remote stony beach together, as though at peace with one another. It depressed the hell out of me. That moment caught and spun in time as the eternal present jarred against me like a grater against a carrot. It was like they had always been together. I thought, where is my together? Then my mind snapped back in clarity knowing this to be just a moment, a place in time, which they moved towards and will move from. He being that charming far too charismatic type will fall for something, someone else, some other dream, just as ardent and forceful. And she being forty he may be her last great love, each moment taking on such resonance she will move towards reclusive solitude, in much the same way Dora Maar did after Picasso. Or perhaps she will be that celebrity type who easily replace one type with another, acting with the same intimacy, the same care, the same conversations."

Rosa   It was a thunderous night, the night we became a community. Within hours buckets of water fell in the village. When the banks of the rivers broke my friends came to stay with me at Illigruum house, which was the highest point available, and very unlikely to flood. After the noise of the storm dissipated we caught ourselves unusually quiet. Staring at the sky reaching for knowledge beyond, with expectant eyes. Perhaps God would make an appearance? Feeling closer to the power and might of Nature we felt closer to the force of God. Hovering in a passage of meaning that forced us to momentarily take their lives very seriously. Everything would be destroyed. They had left everything and they had lost everything.

For years Illigruum House had been empty. Even though Sylvia Plaith had never lived there I romantically imagined it to be her house, the vessel of pain and poetry. Peter called it the Yellow House, and Rufus called it the squat, a word unusual here, because people came, stayed, and paid no money. They never stayed for long, because it was so remote, so distant from the village, perched on such a steep hill, it took an immense amount of energy to leave and come back. Generally people left after a few months. But we would stay for years, holding on to a moment of time that held us together, a moment that had created love. It was the perfect occasion to use change as the possibility to start again. We eight adults became four couples; Rufus and Rebecca, Issy and Allan, Sarah and Peter, and me and James. I had never imagined me, such an outsider, would be coupled with someone that I was so drawn to. But that night he held me close and we wrapped ourselves in a coarse grey blanket, silent and close, wordless-knowledge; "We are together; we are together", my mind hummed, although I knew James would never belong to me, he would be close to me and that then was enough.

Rosa   At first the love I had for James was a very distant love that existed mostly in my mind, which I nestled close to my being, in my mind and heart, rather than the real world. I made no effort to make any real contact. But then the flood happened. It affected all the houses down by the village, as the banks burst due to very heavy rainfall and a problem with the dam. Most people went to the next village, but my new friends came to stay with me. The yellow cottage was too high up to be affected. Often life seems too short, other times it seems too long, but on a day like this, filled with fear and excitement, time unravels and becomes so long that I am scared that I won't have enough energy. Often I have wished that my quite lonely life, which I loved, hadn't been exploded. In many ways I was happier before. But that day I was so exceedingly happy, that I glowed and laughed, felt the joy of being a community, the pleasure of being loved. In many ways this is the paradox of life, as we are not quite sure if it is better to be without the joy of love, because at least then we would not experience the pain of love.

Rosa   When James promised to grow old with me, I thought it so little to ask and so easy for him to give. But a part of me knew that first moment as we stood looking at each other that he would pass in and out of my life as though I was unimportant. That he never saw me as special, and that hurt the most. That night Sarah looked out of the window of the yellow cottage, to down below in the valley. I can see the back of her full and bushy red head even now. The village was a river. It was impossible to get to the yellow cottage now so the group was complete. Rufus, ever practical, had several tins in a rucksack and a couple of bottles of single malt whisky.

Rosa   That night the meal of tin beans and sausages with whisky was delicious. We slept all huddled in my living room, with ourselves and a wood fire as warmth. It was the most exciting, thrilling day of my life and I took every opportunity to gaze at James that I could. The way his ear-length dark hair curled and twisted, his ever-expressionistic eyebrows and his beautiful face, oh and those wonderful watery green-lake eyes that I thought I knew instantaneously. He played the guitar, and a subject met my desire finally. I knew beyond all doubt as he played nervously with depth with questions on questions... metaphysically, with less concern with form, that he was like me. Finally some one like me, I thought. We slept all together, on blankets on the floor, breathing, snoring, fidgeting and wriggling.

Rosa   In the morning, with the bright light of a new day glowing, he whispered that he could see God in my eyes and I prayed silently that God would never leave me, but even then I knew that he would say the same line, see the same in someone else's eyes and I let great big rivers of tears fall from my eyes and onto my cheeks. I knew he would never be mine. Like Picasso, no woman owned him.

Rosa   Perhaps it would be better if the multifaceted nature of our being were reflected in the solidity of our being. Perhaps if we could live for companionship, as an aspect of ourselves with weight and existence much greater than a memory or wish: To leave us, a tangible touchable being to a moment in time. Much more than a hologram, an us. This happens in my favourite movie, Tierra. It's Basque, and shows all the beauty of Basque-ness, the land, and the culture. Angel leaves his deep melancholic side to one woman, and lusty passionate side to another. I take the melancholic side any day. But my idea is beyond having split personality; rather it is about the weight of being. The James that exists beside me is heavy, so much heavier because he is not here in reality, so he becomes heavy, so heavy.

Passages from the Search for Eternal Love

Rosa   I am on the outside looking in. Asking, praying for meaning to be shaped in reality, and the forms in my mind to be the forms in my life. What will I see upon death If I cannot see your dark untidy hair, or puppy-like smile? I hope to see us kissing deeply by the chair. Again, again, un-broken, so often that my heaven becomes this moment, a reality of sorts, and not a question. But it is a question.'Why did you leave me, did you not know that I would be broken in my multi-faceted being, glass not ice. Burden of love, twist aside my un-tranquil heart and make again this reality my warm fold, my nesting blanket. To be in love, to love and receive love, there is nothing that makes time glide more, with clarity and certainty, than love.

Eva   It was so poetic, so beautiful, that I began to think about the possibility that being solo was a pre-requisite for being any kind of artist and I considered my own aloneness. I begin to think also that desire needs distance.

Berkeley's chair

Rosa When you are young you may understand the essence of something but not it's substance; that may take experience. I found Berkeley's argument about the reality of a chair so simple, so obvious, that in many ways it makes perfect sense to say that when we are not observing a chair it may disappear, not be there. It wasn't until much later as I lay on my bed, very ill and confused, that a whole new reality opened up to me, and I understood that Berkeley was just getting us to consider that existence may not be about this hard straightforward reality that we preserve with our senses. I expect that many of you are wondering what happened between me and James - did he reciprocate my love? Well just at the point when my life was at it's best, we made a community with our friendship, and James seemed as in love with me as I with him, life threw me a curve ball and I had a nervous breakdown. It began like a bolt of reality on a road to Damascus.

One day I was rushing around Hebden Bridge, trying to do too many things at once. I was very stressed, but had started to accept stress as a way of being. I crossed the main road hurriedly, and was so inside my head that I didn't notice this enormous red bus heading my way. The bus was moving fast down hill, the driver pressed his horn loudly, but I became petrified and couldn't move. As though paralysed I just stood there watching the bus, expecting to die, but also amazed at my own inability to move. But then without moving a muscle I found myself on the other side of the day. There and then I collapsed in a heap of emotion. I felt terrible. How could I be an expert on being? This question 'How' was ringing loudly in my mind. How did I get on the other side, almost as though I had flown. It was a beautiful amazing thing to have happened, but then I couldn't see the beauty of it. My rational mind wanted to know how it had happened. But I no longer cared about this rational domineering mind, I realised that there was a quieter, open mind that I hadn't listened to before.

My rational mind fought to dominate me, but now I could hear it, and see that it wasn't me, so it tried to destroy me. It was an ugly battle, but a beautiful thing happened. I had been so rational, and I didn't see beauty, only questions. Exhausted, I took to my bed, and found that I didn't have any real reason to get up. Lying there on my bed even stranger things happened. I felt hands on my body, wings under my shoulder blades. Saw people walk through walls. I stayed really still observing these events like an anthropologist, aware that this was possibly a spiritual dimension - but I didn't see these events in a spiritual way, I saw them as mad, and so did my Doctor. I only saw them as spiritual much later when I met Ralph and people like him, who are healers and shamans, and other such wonderful people.

Rosa   Rufus had an explanation but it was sociological, and my questions were large and metaphysical - also I didn't find anything beautiful then, I was so scared, and kept thinking again and again about Berkeley's chair, and how hard I had laughed at the argument for its disappearance, feeling foolish. James was unkind, in his absence. He carried on as though I didn't exist, and eventually fell in love with someone else, as though it didn't matter- as though it didn't matter because I was just a broken person, who might very well stay broken.

The intentional lives of poets

Eva   I walked in the woods, past the talking trees, that nurture and understand these silent thoughts, and found myself at the library, seeking language, considering the lives of poets. One talks of friendship of toilets, alcohol and throwing up, the other of his great love for his children, despite his distance in their lives. The language isn't special, nor are the lives of chatter and cups of tea.

But then I consider that perhaps I am intending my life, with it's roller-coaster ups and downs, with it's heart-felt agony, so that I can reach into my lived humanity and speak of souls, not just my own. As poets, are we intending our lives to be so without reciprocity so that there is more sadness, more emotion to pull apart? I am lonely without you, but its isn't any kind of loneliness, which searches for like-minded people to ask me to dinner, to parties. I find friends so easy, but nothing can appease the absence of a 'him.' I find this shocking even to myself, somehow I intend myself to be here, when I don't have to be here. Or is it that he really is the only other person that I need to see, to be with? Or will I lie down withdrawn, needing him in my mind, so badly that it seems that I am not even happy to see him? I am a lonely writer, a poet with an absent muse and I am coming to believe that my will intends this to nourish this book.

Eva   I remember last Christmas in Brixton, a woman once beautifully exotic now jaded as she drags her suitcase filled with Christmas booze along in a way that is so painful. I help carrying first the fallen items, which I place carefully at the door and then the whole suitcase, rather machismo-ally. I look back; she is so ashamed. I see past the bloated-ness, or overworked kidneys and the alcohol sweat, and see her beautiful dark hair and her multi-ethnic face. I know what she is doing, she has bought herself enough alcohol to stay in, be warm, watch telly and laugh and cry as the alcohol creates a kind of absence to her loneliness, nothing like alcohol for splitting the self into selves, and then you are not alone. I am so sad for us, my generation of poets seemed so possible, most of us knew of our poetic sensibility early but most of us are now sad lonely alcoholics, so sad and lonely that we cannot even make company with each other and year by year become more enclosed in our self-life. By the time my first book of poetry was published I knew no one. I didn't drink, and didn't meet anyone. But then I met Paul.

Eva   My James had been called Paul, and when I decided that I didn't want to drink red wine once a week, shag clumsily and have all those early promises wilfully forgotten, he stopped calling. I hadn't realised that the habit was needed much more than me. I began to realise that seeing deeply was a curse. I saw so much promise and hope in Paul, and he saw another drinking companion. The loss of Paul really knocked me, because the swing of my life pendulum was at maximum and really swung heavily to minimum, and I had never experienced so much pleasure then pain in my life. And I realised there in that moment that everything was transient, and that it probably wasn't worth wanting too much. But I knew how dangerous I myself was, and that I would keep wanting, and wanting, even if that was understanding and knowing, not just having. This woman with the long dark hair and bloated Eskimo face - she had been someone's muse, someone's drinking partner, but the position hadn't elevated her, and he probably hadn't created great work, because our generation of poets focus on their lives, not their work. I remembered Paul - we'd go somewhere, to a party or a bar and we'd be dressed amazingly. He'd go in one direction and I in another.

His voice would echo around the room, with arguments, stories, laughter, and I would be elegant and reflective, eventually we would meet in the middle and his gaze would engulf me, we'd leave, go back to my flat and have the most glorious sex. We were the most magnificent Artistic couple. It was the most magnificent time.

Eva   Two versions of the love paradigm; In one you said love lasts about eighteen months, long enough for a woman to get pregnant, long enough for a baby to become and grow old enough that a woman is able to look after him on her own and on to the next. So many of the men of my generation believe this. I can't believe that the uniqueness of women doesn't bind you to one forever. I imagine though while catapulting from one to another, the uniqueness of one stays in the mind scratching and aching with the mistakes. Another time you said that love could happen, come and go in three months. I gave you a frosty look and said that wasn't love but lust. Then I looked it up and found out that Sylvia Plath and Ted Hughes married after four months. I could have wept, four tumultuous months against a lifetime of loneliness, the kind of loneliness that bites, cold hard-edged truth measured against spinning laughing, loving, spinning, and then you're gone. Love exists in the mind mostly; mostly in the mind, with images, words, longing, hoping wishing against the cold hard truth of months, not years or decades, but months, and months come and go so quickly that they barely matter. Poets do not lead happy lives, as poetry rarely comes from happiness, even when there is talk of it, the poet knows the time of recurrence, the time that shifts, of ebb and flow, loss on loss, and life is much more loss and sorrow than eternal love.

Passages from the Search for Eternal Love

Thoughts of the beloved

Rosa   Although I felt wonderfully happy away from Zennor and Andrew, as time went on I began t realise how still and wise he was. When I wrote telling him I was in love with James, he wrote back saying that someone who fell in love quickly would probably fall out of love even quicker. It wasn't what I wanted to hear, so I ignored it. The community was beautifully sunny at first. We were glad to be together, something poignant had come out of the tragedy of the others losing their homes. Through tragedy we come closest to the bones of our beliefs. Rufus and Rebecca, who had a leaning towards Buddhism, felt relieved of the weight of their possessions and were enthusiastic about us being together as one big happy family.

James was much more dour, as he had lost some very beautiful instruments, though not his skills at making them, so he burrowed away most of the time, creating beauty from wood in the shed. And I blamed James for falling out of love with me - I found his daily moody, grumpiness very unappealing - my disappointment at seeing him daily, as a very self-obsessed conceited person, was hard to hide, as it made me sad and nervous to think that the love of my life, my soul mate, or my eternal love was unpleasant and grumpy much of the time. I'd always seen him from far away, and at a distance he glistened, close up he was grumpy, rude, angry and boring, and though I seemed happy, this was the unspoken truth of my heart, I imagined myself with a warmer, kinder person.

Rosa   I had a lot of work to do. My research focused on the question of being and examined European literature and philosophy - Heidegger, Sartre, de Beauvoir, Ibsen, Strindburg and Ionesco. I really enjoyed researching and writing, and spent much of my time in the library. I shared a room with James. I hated it, having no personal space, and slept badly sharing my bed. But also we had a mistaken desire for love, and desire easily jades. I resented him, I did not love him and he did not love me. We were too polite to bicker or fall out, but even so in the quiet coldness of our relationship we did not move towards compassion or care or understanding, and at best we were nice.

Rosa   Eventually we all had a meeting and we decided that we needed more space. James wanted a workshop and Rufus wanted some therapy rooms. Rebecca wanted a bigger kitchen to make food to sell, and Sarah wanted to start a Steiner school for the children. Pete had ideas to re-train to be a healer. Issy wanted a darkroom. So it was agreed to move from the yellow cottage. James and me hardly spoke, but the group made it clear that we both needed our own rooms. We found an old farm that had a few animals and was run-down, which the owner sold us really cheaply. It was perfect for the children. A little bit too remote perhaps, but a wonderful base. We decided immediately to be vegetarian and keep the few remaining animals as friends. Rufus and Rebecca set to work immediately, and between Rebecca's cakes and chutneys and through Rufus' therapy we had a small income, which was all we needed. Eventually the therapy turned towards retreats and residential courses, and we all played a part. I taught drawing and poetry, and felt happy to fit into being part of a community, and playing my part. I wasn't so happy with my own art and writing, which was dark and angry. It scared me, and I struggled to find an authentic voice. But then I think this struggle became too much and I split into pieces, not knowing who I was, or what the world was. The doctors said it was a nervous breakdown. Everyone in the community was warm and sympathetic, but James avoided me, and eventually I came to realise that although he wouldn't ever say anything, our relationship was over. This compounded everything of my grief, and in my madness I allowed myself to cry, to a weep and wail, to be as sad as sad could be.

Eva   I have one wish, many desires, longings and hopes, but one wish, and that is that in this lifetime as Eva, that I shall meet my true beloved. Often the beauty of God takes the place of the beloved, and we stare mystified and in adoration at the hues of the sky, the warmth of the sun on our skin, or the stillness of the moon. Instead of lying in the arms of our beloved, we lay in the arms of God who understands us omnisciently, loves us, is there for us. I have great faith in the power of the Cosmos, and no God described seems without love or power. Yet it is the loving knowledge of another human that I crave; another person who wants to know me in love; one who can say "ahh, that's so Eva". Who can build a loving knowledge higher than any Babel's tower.

Eva   The myth of Narcissus is probably one of the only Greek myths that most people know; how he looked into a river and fell in love with his own reflection. So perhaps we imagine that our beloved is us - but not us. Loves us like we love ourselves, or perhaps more! I once had a very warm and beautiful Humanities teacher. She was young and independent, and made us girls feel that there was a certain freedom in being educated. As a class we flourished under her tuition. Yet one sad day she announced that she had cancer and would probably die, so she spoke to us in an unusually frank manner. She seemed sad and took time too explain her sadness. She was sad that she would die without knowing her beloved. She was sure he existed, but she didn't have the time to find him, and the reality that she would die without even the knowledge of him, let alone his presence to hold her hand, almost made her life pointless, unlived.

Eva   Last night I looked at a photograph of Jane Morris, taken by Dante Gabriel Rosetti in 1865. Jane was the wife of William Morris, who designed such beautiful fabrics, but was the beloved of Dante. In the photo her wild frizzy hair is momentarily tamed, perhaps by Dante in a gentle caress. He painted her again and again, never tiring of her, as many artists tire of their muses, moving on unkindly and aggressively. The pretence of love is something that greatly annoys me, and in the moment of death saddened my humanities teacher.

I had plenty of time to let go of London, the life I had with Paul. One of my main regrets was my inability to see change and misfortunes as a real opportunity for change and happiness. Lacking adaptation, fearing change, I put most of my energy into conforming, rarely seeing that shifts are wonderful opportunities for change; ways to move closer to truths. To move closer to the lives we hope for. Allowing imagination to give way to the unexpected.

Rosa   A day is a brief period of time. So brief that perhaps the only way we can make progress from one day to another is by having dramatic things happen: Some happy, some sad. 'Dramatic' means emotions. Perhaps we need to educate ourselves about emotions. Understanding the way life feels - how to react to have the outcomes we most desire. Knowing what we desire. Which perhaps is the hardest thing. Prayer in a sense is about this. A way of getting to know ourselves and about what we want to happen. Often we say 'I want you to love me and never leave', and then when we get this it feels wrong and we project something else, we have to learn to love, and learn through love.

Eva   I knew exactly what Rosa meant. I had never given Paul precise and clear signs of love, fearing my own adoration, feeling it as a whole, as a loss, as a weakness. But desiring so much. Hoping for so much. The dichotomy left such confusion.

Paul had never been mine, a fact that he often displayed. But one day he could have been. There we were, at the same exhibition. I hadn't expected to see him. He sent me an email but I said I was in Spain, which was true. But I made it sound like I was there still but I had been back for a while, as things no longer worked with my Basque lover as I loved his country more than him. He stood behind me and rolled my name out, his voice low and moist. I turned around and saw that illness had really aged him. His beautiful black hair was thin but his orange-brown eyes were very loving. Before they had been lusty and I knew he could be mine. But there would be no more parties, no more art-couple. We would have to settle down and get to know each other. Eight years later, seemed eight years too late, I had been ready in New York, but now I had been alone too long and knew him only as an idea, a longing, there was no space for him as a reality. He chased me around the room, moving to wherever I moved to. Eventually I gave him the slip and later changed my email.

Eva   Forgetting about Paul I am reminded of Anthony. Anthony was one of the first people I met at University. It was a mad, frenzied time, as people tried to couple, to form groups. One day Anthony invited me to be in a film with him. It involved sitting around drinking and looking bohemian. Apparently I wasn't bohemian enough, or perhaps the wrong type, so first we went to his house to pick up a beautiful black waistcoat. I fancied Anthony. I loved his voice, deep and serious. He looked like he enjoyed life, particularly sex. I was looking forward to it. So was he. He lived in a squat, and though the waistcoat was immaculate, the house was a rubbish dump. It wasn't that it was a squat. Most of the people I knew lived in a squat. It was uncared for. I turned off Anthony, I knew he would be needy, and indeed he was. We drank loads of vodka, but nothing he did could seduce me. I was turned off. There was always a flirtation, and one day, we kissed wildly in the night in a garden, away from a party, and had wild athletic sex. He loved my legs. But in the morning he was silent. I left it to him. Nothing happened, as if paying me back for the night he couldn't seduce me he created a nothing. I gave him back his waistcoat. Eventually we met in a café. He told me he didn't want a relationship. I loved the release, it didn't hurt at all.

The waiting, hoping, oh that hurt loads. Eventually we left University. After a couple of months he rang me, spoke of desire, serendipity brought us together again and again, but I had spent too many heartbroken months, it was too late. What did I mean by this? I meant that he left me hurt, myself undoing, he left me unhappy and that kind of hurt wasn't love. I wanted only love, desire was easy, given the right circumstance anyone was desirable, there was nothing special, nothing binding, and life is short, the days of love, very short.

Rosa It was very damp in new Illigruum house. The stones it was built from stayed part of nature. No-one expected to create a community there, but having lost everything it seemed stupid not to try to continue, but rather to move forward through a stream of serendipity that created a new thread of future, and a new place in time. Little by little we felt the trickle of perceptual change, being together experiencing the same just made everything much easier to bear, and we wondered why they hadn't thought to do it earlier, without the force of nature, to become a family.

That first night is still impossible to describe, the fission of changing energy, of me and James no longer a couple.

Everything was sorted, balanced, I knew that James would never belong to me, he never belonged to anyone, but it hurt enormously when Peter's sister Angela came to stay and unhappily for me when she left, took James with her to France. I saw their love, even before it happened, like a trail of melting light, and you could have called me paranoid, but I knew from the moment they met I ceased to be special, above everything, that hurt the most, that next to Angela, against her lightness, her joy, her long blonde hair, her freeness, I was a dark shadow, a deep unpleasant pool of anxiety. But no one questioned the way that James slipped into the spare room with Angela. Fearing the labels of madness, people rarely create scenes. That just happens in movies. Eventually they left and I stayed, sad and hurt, but still part of a family. During these days our gathering spoke mostly about how to start a peace revolution. Semantics mixed with banana bread, change without drama, without violence.

We made bread, cakes and occasional dinners for the local community, which we sold in one of the outbuildings, which became a very homely café, and that made all the money we needed because we had happiness without spending. Even I with my wound was happy. But it was a niggling wound that would open very easily, for it was tender, tender because love makes tender wounds.

Passages from the Search for Eternal Love

Platonic Love

Rosa   What I know of Plato relates hardly to love. I know of his dusty old forms, rigid and unchangeable. Then there is a love, which we call Platonic, often used when we care about someone but we do not adore them, a love which relates to the love in which we do not wish to gasp someone, to suffocate them in the having of them, but love in wanting the best for them even if that means not seeing them. How to reflect about how the world spins past so fast and yet a movement so far from linear, sometimes breathlessly rides over time, still, silent, scared.

To be in this world without making a difference, or making a child seems too pointless. To be in this world without being loved, seems even more pointless. But as the years spun past and I saw no more of James, yet he did not occupy my mind less. Solid thoughts sounded in my mind of present happenings. I had dialogues with the trees; they told me the most beautiful things and my heart was filled. In many ways I hoped not to see him again, but only to fill my mind with him, my platonic love was not about him, it was of him, of him with me, and it mattered not if the real man married Angela and they had children, I had the Platonic James, who occupied my heart and mind.

Eva   When my mother went to work the young girl from next door used to come and read me stories, make us sweet milk, and sometimes tell me of her boyfriends, who often changed yet in the describing seemed to be the same person, an idol. Later love obsessed me. I focused on those subtle feelings that spoke the word 'love', and wondered how we knew we were with the right person, existing closely, tightly together against the world.

I had no real framework for that kind of closeness, mine was a single working mum, and I began to believe that this inhibited me greatly. Because perhaps these young girl's stories were my only framework; dark nights in the park, of looking upwards and seeing his eyes glow, of desire and longing. That early hopeful stage became something I expected and wanted to be a constant. I knew no dullness, just stars and stars...

Rosa   It was great studying literature and philosophy, and while philosophy helped to encase my thinking in eloquence I read some wonderful works of literature by Kafka, Ibsen, Strindberg, Rilke, Sartre and Kierkegaard. And felt after that it was really possible to communicate - not just to shout or persuade, but also to seek to understand each other. Yet the together aspect of being just didn't seem possible. I had none of the loneliness of childhood, but I dreaded old age in a small dingy flat, watching out of windows, watching. I was no longer young and had yet to meet the people that I read about in literature. The reason love obsessed me; the reason I started "learning through love" was that I rarely saw examples of it. I knew many people alone who longed for it and many people together who whether they dared to show it or not were deeply unhappy.

Passages from the Search for Eternal Love

Rosa At university I met a wonderfully kind Irish man, who dressed as though he was a nineteenth century poet. He wore beautiful old suits, with waistcoats, and cravats. The first day we met he told his best friend that he was going to marry me. It wasn't true. We had the most marvellous friendship. Spending days and days walking, reading, going to readings, and watching plays. We however could make the physical aspect of our love sing.

I hated to see his beautiful face contorted in passion and desire, it put me off him. I tried to explain to him. He thought I didn't desire him, but this wasn't true, I just didn't desire the way he expressed desire. I couldn't relax and release my desire. I think we knew each other too well, and sex seems much better when you don't know too much about each other. I loved the awkwardness of James. He gave so much effort and during the release was truly beautiful.

I have seen many men rise above my body awkwardly contorted, their mouths twisted, and the ones I found impossible to see again were the ones who repelled me when they released their jouissance. There was no knowing who might repel or attract by mere conversation or looking, one had to get to that moment of release to know. I'm sure it was instinct, animal, because only with those that looked beautiful, happy to be doing the most bizarre of all things, could I really be myself and let go, be clumsy, taste, push, claw, love and finally glow.

Eva I look outside to the warm dark night. I am getting old - nearly forty - and though I hold Paul as a great love, I will not allow him to be my greatest love, that would diminish this life to something small and unimportant, and in that moment I let go of Paul. He isn't even interesting enough to hold as a platonic love. He is just someone with whom I felt an enormous amount of desire, who made me feel like a goddess and a muse, who inspired me to be what I thought I was. No, my greatest love would have to inspire me to be an amazing person - what I longed to be in the crevices of myself, the dark corners, the aspects of light, and I hadn't come across him yet.

Passages from the Search for Eternal Love

The death of self in the couple

Rosa Much as I loved James with every aspect of my being, the ache of abandonment, the stabbing wounds of embarrassment and the fear of being on my own slowly became nothing, replaced instead by a self that I remembered and preferred, an alone self. My alone self was far more interesting, she watched space and time, took an existential approach to being, was far more optimistic, far less sad, and I was far happier to have her back than I would have been to have James, this man who promised nothing and gave so little.

Rosa While waiting to see the psychiatrist, I observe a couple. She was of a similar age and ethnicity to me, and while she had vibrancy about her, she neglected aspects of looking after herself. Her skin suffered dehydration and had dry patches. Her hair was bundled into a rather dull frizzy ponytail. Her clothes while not shabby lacked imagination and sensuality; a man's tracksuit bottom, and boring coat. The worst was the frothy way words slipped from her mouth, as she lacked many teeth.

As I watched her interact with her partner it became obvious why she neglected herself. He took up ever moment of her time. If she wasn't talking to him directly, she was finding someone, anyone in the waiting room to talk to about him. I was there as long as she and nothing but him left her mouth. He sat opposite, glad to be so important. I gathered that once he would have been the most handsome of the group, but drugs, alcohol and his ego had stripped him of this, but the frisson of past attractiveness stayed with him and despite his toothlessness and matted hair she was so proud of her man.

Rosa   He reminded me of James and for the first time since he left me I became so glad that he had left me, left me empty, ready to begin again.
More than anything I began to see relationships as opportunities to learn enormously about myself, about us. After James I decided that I would walk a straight path, the path of God I called it. It was the path that would exist if everything were predetermined. It meant that I no longer met forked paths, infinite decisions, but would do exactly what I thought God would want from me. It took away layers of anxiety and doubt, fear and self-blame. One of the things I learnt at this time was from watching, over and over, one of the children's Spiderman films.

Leon watched it over and over gain and though he was only two and a half he knew some of the text off by heart. The worst character, the weakest, silliest and least likeable character was like me. He fell in love after one date, persisted even when this love was unrequited, was needy. Anything was OK but not to be needy, not to want and ache and need, and need. But surely we were all like this? Wasn't it love? I began to realise that life was about playing, making moves, creating personas, holding onto power, and all these insights, all this possibility was possible because I lived without love, without another. Without thoughts of James my mind swelled, became my best friend, and from then on I decided that I would not be a couple again. I would not let my teeth rot away in my mouth from self-neglect, and I would not let my every thought spin on another. It is through love that we can understand each other and the world, as we struggle to find each other, and be there in a way that demands so much compromise and so much change, often stepping outside our comfort zones to find what will change our lives for the better and give us hope. Without love, we would risk nothing, lose nothing, know nothing. That became really apparent as we started to form the community.

I stopped going to university and gave the time I would have been studying to teaching the four children. It seemed appropriate, as I was a scholar without children. Giving the parents a break. Eventually though the children went back to school and I had to seek a new place in the community. I found myself with clay, making at first simple vessels for Rebecca's lovely cakes and pickles. Eventually I converted one of the smaller outbuildings into a very cosy studio. I spent the earlier part of the day going for walks in the woods, and then reading , and after we all met and had lunch the afternoon was for art. I stuck with clay, though sometimes I used it for casting larger pieces. I came to spend a lot of time by myself, and this spilled into the rest of my life. I loved walking by myself, no longer fearful of the rocky damp nature that surrounded our new Illigruum House. I no longer hungered for another, I had become my other. I sometimes thought of James, but no longer hungered for him passionately. Instead of seeing his eyes, his beautiful dark hair, I saw a man who wanted to damage the best part of me, my capacity to love

- I was angry, sad and eventually relieved. The timing of this was brilliant, because soon I would have a new pair of eyes to focus my mind on - a genuinely kind person - Ralph.

The desert of my being

Rosa   In many ways it is better to hope and try in love, again and again. The spark of love many be platonic and kind, friendship rather than wild abandoned lust, so the trail of the initial spark may be like the warm embers of the night's fire, quietly constant, no roar in sight- but still it is love. Perhaps we place too much emphasis on that special love, with time to share? But if life is eternal, rather to share it with someone known, and knowing than being alone! Being alone is perhaps the best state to be present. Having your heart broken is perhaps the best beginning life can afford. But if life is eternal, then everyone wants to meet that person who can love them best.

Rosa   By the time I was nearly forty, the children in the community were grown, and I could no longer gain comfort from their innocence. It was time to have a child of my own. I hadn't been alone all that time, but hadn't found someone who I could see myself sharing my life with. I started to realise that I would have to leave Illigruum house, its comfort and solidity and go back to the desert of my being.

To see land again as an outstretched infinite possibility; to stumble in recklessness and joy. I decided to travel to France and took the hovercraft, a speedy if somewhat sterile experience, and met no one. Dieppe, however, was a lovely seaside town, with a busy market, and a real centre. I booked into a hotel with uneven floors, low beamed ceilings, and delicious food. The majority of people who came to the hotel Ramone came to eat at lunch, a two-hour festival of soft pork and bean stews, cheese and wine. I spoke in French, shy and quiet as though the poetic language was revealing my real personality. I thought I would however not meet anyone. Eventually after a week I met a man who recognised I was English from the English speaking edition of Herman Hesse's Steppenwolf.

Rosa   "To read Hesse you really have to learn German". The accent sounded American, the face was wide open and beautiful, his eyes aqua green, a colour that was unusual in eyes.
"I have give all my language brain to French, and while I think German is my favourite language, my brain thinks it too difficult", I said.

The conversation went on like this, mildly intellectual and flirtatious, and subtly revealing until Ralph revealed something much more important. He was heading South to a place on the border between France and Spain, for a meeting of spiritual awakening, the energy of which would inspire all of us to change the world, in the very best way. I was hooked on the beauty of Ralph and the seriousness of his mission. I was shocked however when he said that it would be best if we didn't travel together. We got on so well together, that I had a co-dependent relationship. Luckily for me though, I knew that this was the grasping side of my being, and I listened to the other side which was just so happy to be travelling on my own to something so exciting and promising. He did not give a reason, and I realised that this was a different quality of Being. He was somehow more authentic. Instead he gave me a piece of paper with precise instructions on how to reach Bearn. I considered not going, but knew that I had to and as soon as I was on the train in an empty carriage for a 9-hour journey I realised it was the most amazing experience. I didn't have someone to cling to, so I felt the moments of time, the countryside was beautiful, and I began to be in the desert of my being, in stillness while moving. I realised that I felt that I was going home, while becoming, creating myself and unravelling myself, I started to realise that I was never really myself when with others, I lost the voice of my mind.

I needed to be alone in the stillness to hear and know and really know myself, my consciousness. As the train approached the green and curvaceous mountains of the Basque area I vowed that I would try to find a way of keeping this journey with me, of never letting this me disappear. To not attach myself to the beauty of another but stay in the silence and let my voice talk, that voice that would become known if you are alone in a desert, a desert that seems to stretch out to infinity. The main problem that faces us all in the desert of our being is boredom, that kind that always longs for the threshold of excitement; I wanted to know truth not excitement, not a bubbling champagne, but cold pure water.

The past perhaps is a better place to play and analyse; no future hunger, rather longing and remorse. I took my mind back to that first year at Illigruum house when everyone but James and me had gone to spend Xmas with relatives. We busied ourselves with chores, collecting wood, cleaning with care and making wholesome meals.

Doing these activities together made me feel closer to him. We cuddled on the old sofas and marvelled at the warmth and character of the open fire, often falling asleep there, wrapped together. James however was already having thoughts of someone else and as soon as I saw her I knew of their intimacy and care. Angela had a forest of hair, and a beautifully sculptured face, her smile was wide and confidant, her eyes a misty blue.

She his imagination, and more than that she was the singer that James had always dreamt would accompany his playing. I was subdued at the New Years party, hardly there and then just at the time when everyone was looking for someone to kiss, they were together. I walked through the woods alone, silently conversing with God as to why there was always someone better than me, as to why I was not good enough. I didn't have my answer then, I had it now, on that train journey through the French Basque area, through the green mountains to meet Ralph, a man whom I shared very little conversation with, but knew instantly, and was meeting head on in that knowing. I was reminded that God's plan is a broad one embracing all of time, all our lives, I was at last able to thank God for the unpleasant ending with James. Yet there was more I recognised; those wet deep green mountains cuddling the beautiful moist grey sky in myriad and multiples. I knew that I had been to the Basque Country in a dream. The kind of lucid dream you have when you have to make decisions – the life-changing sort. I remembered I was a part of the mountain, stillness in all stillness, as if rock, because there was a sense of being trapped. Next thing I hard a voice of a child singing, that was so beautiful, there was power in its beauty. It released me and I too became a child, skipping, running, and singing.

It was true; I was becoming a child, following possibility with earnest trust and hope. Taking a train to a place I didn't know, to meet a man I didn't know. Everything was based on feeling, the intuitive sort. For the first time I believed that I could follow my intuition and all the possibility it opened up.

The eternal recurrence

Rosa   Just a moment, there caught in your time, caught in mine, it can reccur over and over again. The moment that I caught myself in Cambio-les bains for lunch is a pivotal moment. As the train pulled into Cambio-les-bains, I heard a voice in my head as loud and clear as if someone next to me was talking. I said plain and clear, 'Get off now. Don't think about it, just get off'. I wasn't frightened at all. I no longer thought that seeing a psychiatrist was the answer, but thought of voices as me, or my ancestors trying to communicate. I decided to get off for some lunch. It was a beautiful village. Nestled in the mountains, with views everywhere you turned. I found myself along with the whole village at the hotel having the set menu of pork and beans, cheese and wine.

There was so much happiness here and it wasn't the wine. The control factor that was about the rest of Europe seemed absent, people seemed to more or less have forged themselves and the layered conformism was unnecessary as there was a place for everyone. I loved it, but had to continue the train journey, I had agreed to meet Ralph in Bearn at a hostel there, it wasn't far, just another 20 minutes on the train but there wasn't another train, not until tomorrow.

Rosa   I didn't panic like I would have done in the past but simply took a room at the hotel. The next train was in the morning. I planned to relax in my room, but once I stated wandering around this pretty village with its Basque houses made traditionally in black white and red, market square and gothic church, it was too interesting. Thirsty, I stopped in a small bar, it was dark and beatnik, something like a sixties den and they were playing sixties folk music. When I asked for a glass of red wine, I didn't notice at first that the bartender was James. He had changed, and was very bloated from unhappiness and red wine. He smiled and seemed pleased to see me and I returned that smile. We chatted for a while about Illigruum House, and I told him that he was always welcome back, and I stayed a while to hear his fluid folk music on the guitar, but neither of us tried to make something happen. I listened and he played. After he stayed in the bar and drank, and I slept well in a soft comfortable bed, and the only signifier to our great love affair was in our eyes.

Eva   Recently because of 'learning through love' I have started a night journal, to make tangible the whisperings in my head. Clarity is passing through me: I actually know my desires. Before this journal, I was never sure what I wanted from life, who I wanted to be, would let life make all the choices for me, even if that meant just flowing back and forth and not really going somewhere. My best friends said that the problem was that I was too intelligent for the men I dated. But only recently I realised how many different intelligences there are- to let go, when everything is telling you to hold on was an emotional intelligence that was so necessary. Here at Illigrum house I am for the first time ever at a place of stillness. I am not in a relationship. I feel breath and wind around me; I am getting to know my kingdom, getting to know myself. And with that everything takes on less meaning, even the spinning of time, of my personal history, reminding me of a painful past, even they are swallowed up by Rosa's stories, and the presence of mountains and grey skies. I am alive.

Passages from the Search for Eternal Love

Abundance and presence

Rosa   I wasn't expecting much more to happen on the way to Bearn. I got on the train the next morning, knowing that all the growth that had happened for James and me would not have been possible had we been together. I had learnt so much, talking with the trees in the stillness of my workshop, moulding and forming clay, painting and being. Yet as I sat down on the train I found myself drawn to a very open, powerful woman, with short brightly coloured hair.

She said that her name was Tiffany and that she too was on her way to the Caves of Bearn for a spiritual meeting. She knew a lot more about it than me, and I was happy to be filled in on the history of this meeting. It had begun as a group of people meeting to dance ecstatically, in Brixton. The group grew bigger and found that many members were healers and creatives, and so they moved to a church in Vauxhall. The energy generated by this group of dancers was so healing, so powerful that they knew that they could change the world for better. So they were meeting in the Caves, inviting anyone along who had a similar energy and willingness to make the world a better place. I actually felt ashamed by how little I knew so I asked her to tell me, and this is what she said.

Rosa   "I lived in a small village in England. You know the kind you long to escape from. To get to some big city like London, Paris or New York. My mum was French so as soon as I could I went to the Sorbonne in Paris to learn philosophy. It was a great place to hang out in, but it was all words and concepts. I found that these great concepts, while interesting, didn't relate to that small little village girl that I was and that I returned to at dusk, while all alone. I asked too many questions and my tutors looked at me as if I was a nuisance. So I gave up my studies and began working in a shop that sold spiritual books, crystals etc in the village where I grew up. These no longer seemed like trinkets. I found here in this small shop all the answers to the questions that I had and more. I learned about abundance, this is the concept that whatever you want, you first have to give. I learned that through creative visualisation we can create the possibilities that we long for. I learnt that we have to shape our desires, and then as prayers they will come true, perhaps not when we expected, so we have to make sure that these desires are really what we went. I learnt to float on life, to relinquish and not strive. So now I am here on the way to the groats in Bearn for one of the biggest spiritual meetings.

I asked her if she had met Ralph. She smiled then said. "He is very lovely, beautiful isn't he? He energises and gives unselfishly"
I felt jealous as though Ralph was mine, to own, to possess, in the way that I had wanted James. Sensing my thoughts she corrected them.
"He is beautiful because he knows, not because he is", she said
And I knew exactly what she meant.

Eva   I once lived in Camden with a man who was full of possibility. Being with him so much happened; visiting flamenco bars to watch a large red haired passionate dancer, being part of a small jazz-funk scene, and visiting old dusty gay bars late at night to the early hours. I left him because I didn't desire him, although it was the best partnership. I just liked to be with him- like a best friend, and that wasn't enough for me. I wanted to find my eternal love. He was so angry that he cut off all contact, and my social life shrivelled to nothing. It was then that I experienced the void for the first time - I wanted to not exist, to disappear because living each day was so painful.

I didn't want to hurt myself, but softly squeeze the life from me - because to live without ever coming close to meeting my eternal love was not a life at all. But Rosa was saying something, in the story of the train journey now I was coming close to hearing that there was something else beyond having that person close to you, something spiritual that would connect me to the eternal rather than meeting one man who would be my eternal. The key was perhaps abundance; to gain love we have to give love. This concept gave me breath for the first time, because I realised I had a lot of love to give, that I could keep on giving even if it didn't seem that it was returned in a reciprocal way, just to give and keep on giving.

Eternal love

Rosa   As we travelled, we both became silent and I wrote Ralph this love letter -

You are such a beautiful person - all the good inside radiates from your being. I see how your eyes are aqua-blue in dull artificial light, but a soft smoky grey in the sunshine. How the different facets of your personality wane from rebellion to conformity with kind acceptance of yourself. How you face changes so amazingly with the most wondrous of expressions. Your beautiful expressions often glow with luminosity. I love that you have both the capacity to be still and present, even when you are uncomfortable. But in your natural state you are so alive, so sexy, then you appear magical. I love that you are very kind and compassionate, that you are human and fallible.

Eva   This year I saw a film when a woman held her dying love in her arms, as a baby, and I then by coincidence read that Simone de Beauvoir held her life-long love in her arms while he died. She wanted to lie next to him under the sheets but he was covered in gangrene from his festering bedsores. The thing that depresses me most about the cinema is that it plays with time in a rather heartless way. The theatre tends to show you real time, but cinema where it can shows birth and death as short moments of stills spun really fast. A birth can follow to old age and death in moments. It makes me feel so insignificant to the world and its being, when really I want to be really significant. I want to change the world, because it isn't kind enough to us, and cinema makes our vision even more diminished for most of us, nearly all of us are bit parts that come and go with no blue plaque saying we lived here or there, with no biography book. It's so; I was here and now I'm gone. The best we can do to be remembered is to have children, and for them to have children. Our love stories could be days, months, years but no more. And in these ungenerous special moments we have to love. I wanted to love and be loved so much, but it had to be true, but all I seemed to have were adventures. I have always wanted to change the world too, but all I seemed to have managed is envy, bitterness, guilt and regret.

I wanted to be a spiritual leader who made things better, but all I had was madness, voices, whispers, and occasional glimpses of parallel universes. I didn't want power or influence but just possibility, but more and more I came to see and feel that possibility only comes with deep aloneness... from spending time alone, thoughtful, sad, and sometimes happy but mostly just listening and trying to understand.

Rosa I walked around Cambio-les-bains and felt the strong sense of Déjà vu. That church tarnished and sooty, I knew, the little corner with the boulangerie, butchers and small wine bar I knew before. Yet it wasn't a comfortable sensation; it nagged at my confidence. When I saw James at the bar my heart leapt. The visceral attraction I still had for him made me want to weep. Here I was feeling something so strong that not even the beauty of Ralph could disconnect. In seeing him I felt him, I remembered holding him, I remembered knowing him, why was this beautiful energy not returned? When he moved from the bar and picked up his guitar, I felt like running but I stayed and listened to his sad songs. He knew loneliness as I did, how wonderful it was to yearn, how sad it was not to share. The best song was about a piece of paper mocking a pen, "There's no poetry between us, said the paper to the pen". Yes it was true, love was too many petty, lying arguments and not enough, "You are beautiful", "You make me happy". That night there were so few of us in the bar, that I felt that James played for me, yet I felt awkward. As James walked me to my hotel I took the opportunity to be frank.

Rosa   "Why did you hurt me in such an obvious painful way, treat me as if I was a broken person, no longer worthy of your love?" I asked James.
"When I was young"; it was true we had been young. He was now quite round and his hair was no longer heavy, but his murky green eyes had deepened from experience and were thrilling to look into.

"When I was young I lived by an unspoken manifesto; live life freely, without regret. To accept whatever came my way. Angela was the type of woman I always expected I'd be with. Whereas you were too distant- thinking made you cold, she was warm. I needed warmth then. Now I would find it suffocating. We change. I've changed. "

Rosa   He wanted to try again, but in meeting Ralph, I was inspired to want more. I had to go to Bearn and see Ralph and make way for the opportunity to be something much greater than me, that

might fulfil my hopes to change the world. I said
"James, what you offer is vague and non-committal and while I don't want to suffocate myself, much of what I like about myself is my aloneness. I love you deeply and would only accept something reciprocal. I was so hurt by the way you didn't talk to me and explain. It was as though I was not important enough, special enough, for certain words. That hurt more than anything. I have met someone else, someone I hardly know, who will change my life. I have a visceral tangible love, that wants to hold you, lie by you, smell you, but I feel deep down that you don't yet share that, and I feel too old to let you practice love on me."

James said nothing but took me to my room anyway and kissed me lightly.
" Will you come to Bearn?" I asked
He said that he might and asked 'Do you believe it's true that this meeting will change the world?'
"Yes", I said softly. "But what I know about change is that it is mucky, dangerous. That it is a violence of sorts. Change scares the leaders of the world, because although they know that reality is broken, like a broken vase, they'd rather keep fixing it than let it extend to its broken state and become what we do not know."

Mad love

Eva   What I know most about love swings somewhere between that which is so mundane, whilst in it you fear you will die of it and L'amour fou, madness that makes no sense but destroys, through fear, through truth... Camille Claudel knew she was not the same as Rodin, no matter what he said to convince him. To make her art she tapped into her madness again and again, at first drawing strength and beauty and then she allowed herself to go to the ugly space, danger, poverty, loss and fear. Rodin had no time for this type of life as does most of the world. He hovered somewhere above or below his madness but never in it, never consumed.

How often I have heard men say they are the same as me, and then give me the label free spirit or such. Luckily for me I know the pendulum swings back and forth, that it hovers, is still; I know that nothing, not the wildest love, not even the most mundane, is only the love caught on celluloid, or in the pages of a book that resembles Noah's arch all the rest comes and goes, like weather comes and goes. This knowledge, this grand metaphor gives me hope again and again. But now I wish to know something else about love, something eternal about love; perhaps you do too, can we find our eternal love, that person we have known through time and space, that stands beside us, invisible but there in our dreams, or is it this search that turns our love fou, making folly, how can you want to leave when life is so short, and time is already passing, passing...So I asked you about boredom and you said, "You mean why do I get bored with my relationships? Well I would also get bored from eating steak every day". And although I love you we live in separate universes, they are not even parallel. I see boredom as my best teacher, from him I learn more about myself, the world, us. From him my writing flows, my feelings gush, I am alive. I cause no mischief. I wish not to escape. In boredom I see no misery. Perhaps not steak…certainly not peas but I could eat rice every day if needs must and the everydayness of being is the steak surely and this is life, life we do every day.

Eva   I have been mad several times, and in being mad I have learnt that there is insight if I don't become too fearful. Mad is not a place I think everyone should experience but I know that mad is much the same as death or dreams and these we all experience. Often the sanity of the day is containment, and much is about conformity. But I have learnt that if we sleep little through stress and fear we travel on a different river, and in doing so see different sights, or perhaps they are the same but no longer conform quite so rigidly.

I think I have seen your love, and hoped for it even more, yet if it is not returned, would that make me mad? Often love is returned, but as lust without care. So as in abundance I am deepening my love, as in care for everyone, and in deepening I need your love less, and I am no longer mad. I need it because it is, it is because abundance makes it so, and so there is nothing to lose or grasp, I can just watch and experience, and be. I was learning so much from

Rosa, but now as with any love story I was hoping to know if either James or Ralph was her true love, whether she was to give up on love. I slept thinking about her, and myself, and I was glad that Paul was gone from my love, because he hardly knew me at all, and that the best, the most delicious part of love, was the knowing, to be known, to know.

Rosa   At the hostel in Bearn it seemed that everyone there was there for the spiritual meeting. Everyone, campers and those of us crammed in shared rooms gathered for lunch, and ate our vegetarian supper heartily, as we talked and shared. Afterwards I found myself like many others wandering around the grounds, walking around trees, and catching the sun on the bright green grass. It was a meeting, and all sorts were there. Hippie types in tie-died purple, gothic hippies in flowing black, yogi types in loose brightly coloured plain and simple robes, scholar types in tight jeans and leather, all types, meeting.

Rosa   The trouble with the inherited world we are born into is that it seems unshakable, unmovable. All the meetings I've ever been to are about words, and in those words is the language of doing, as if nothing can happen without those doing, action words. It always seems to be aggressive, fast and frenetic. But this meeting was a meeting of intention. It carried on this way, as we all gathered at the caves in Bearn, in the morning, there in our European ancestors' first homes, there was little speaking, no proposing, this was no revolution, no cue. Everyone knew why they were there, to make the transition from one reality to another. Transitions were usually made with anger and revolution; to change the world one had to blame the past, overthrow it, and become the new. There in the oldest homes of our European ancestors, we were making the new, and this meeting was to be the birth canal of the Now. A way to build upon the radicalism we started with music and dance. We danced and danced, looked at each other, loved each other, and hoped for the best, the very best, and as we danced we became a Sanga. We would heal each other, all types of healers were there, some were Reiki masters and spiritual healers, psychologists, Yoga Teachers practitioners of all kinds, and in dancing this way we would become aware of our ancestors and guides who knew the way, our path. Learning to listen to their murmurings, the murmurings of the trees, the murmurings of our minds. There I met Ralph again, and without talking, we smiled and danced.

Eva   I was stilled wanting to know more about the romantic love than the meeting, but that night I had a dream that unsettled me and I began to think deeply. In the dream I spoke to death. I had never once believed that death would be an entity, but a process, but here, as in some Buddhist doctrine death was a being, talking to me, and as I awoke I found myself reflecting on Paul and others who I have loved who suffer from drinking too much.

Eva   My best and kindest friends have always had problems with alcohol. And while loving these people so deeply, I have loathed them for their addiction, which makes them suffer and makes them make others suffer; their inability to fly high, like me and sink low, without anything to make it more fun or exciting, just my soul, my voice and my need to understand. Once I was in a private hospital, and there amongst so many recovering people I felt I was in an artistic community. But then a nurse broke that spell when she took me to a ward where people were dying from alcoholism, she showed me tumours as big as cats, cadaverous people dying whom no one visited. People dying in the most extreme pain because of their addictions. Why she did this I don't know. But the building blocks of my life are about making connections between what happens in my life, and my parallel universes. One woman whose tumour seemed as large as her said, "She's staring at me", I think as if to say why, and it is only today that there is a possibility that perhaps I was the only person there able to see these tumours!

Eva   I began to see that all my past lovers had also been addicts. The truth is that my addict friends and lovers have hurt me so much, not understanding where I go without verbosity, hilarity, with just intensity as my only friend. I find this brave. I live in an area where many lost and discarded artists live. There are different areas. The sad alcoholics hide in one corner, the verbose in another, many others limbless struggle around in wheel chairs, still drinking, you don't see them for long. How creative they are, were, and how well they create dramas and events with this creativity. I however felt beyond this able to be strong without drink. Where did this come from? Had the meeting in the Grotes passed on a kind of possibility to me? So far from my life, my being- Was the meeting in the Grotes de Bearn, not a rescue but a healing, like a domino flicking and touching another?

Rosa   When the dancing stopped, I took my bottle of water and settled under a tree. For a while I watched the light and shadows settle and change. Then I found that I had company; it was Ralph.

"Isn't it amazing to be here, meeting by word of mouth, but still certain to meet each other", he said warmly. I tried to stand, but he settled on the ground and I next him.
"I know it might seem odd, but what happens next?"

Rosa   "Good question. We are having an event where proven and powerful healers are aiming to heal people of their addictions. Often people addicted are very intuitive people, creative people who find themselves tapping into the spirit world for their art, but because they haven't been trained like healers or mediums often they take on spirits they can't handle who reassure them only when they are drunk or out of it, so that's the state they want to stay in. It stops them from feeling rubbish about themselves. But they cause a lot of harm when they're out of it and that makes them feel more rubbish in a vicious, unkind and destructive way of being.

Some of the healers know how to take on these bad energies and get people back to the neutral place where they were when children, and then create ways that the person feels and is protected, can create without being attacked by negativity, yet still intuitive and creative."

Rosa "It sounds amazing"

"There's this Korean woman who heals by dancing. She gets into a trance when she's dancing and then enters the body of the addict and tackles the negative spirits head on. It's very powerful to watch, I think we all gain healing by watching, by just being part of the ceremony".

"I think that in many ways our ancestor knew more than us". Ralph nodded his head in agreement.

"Yes, I always thought that this idea of a progressive society was deeply flawed if the majority in the world suffered in poverty and starvation; if women spend the majority of the day finding enough water to stay alive; if people are allowed to be cruel to each other without reproach; if the planet is littered in rubbish. I think for a while that things will swing backwards, and no amount of trying to fix it will help, because it's broken for a reason."

Rosa There was a long silence between me and Ralph as we simply felt the breeze, heard its song through the branches and leaves of the trees and allowed the stillness to embrace us. I was aware of the niggles in my mind that were reproachful and negative, but I no longer thought of them as my niggles but rather as negative murmurings left over from the past of love and regret. I no longer felt myself to be in an ocean of emotion, but simply and peacefully sitting next to a tree, with a friend. Looking forward to more dances and more healing.

The Korean woman looked like a shaman that was for sure, with her heavy headdress, she appeared like a human bird, and I would not be surprised if she suddenly took flight. She seemed to be singing and dancing for herself, as though she tried to ignore the fact that we were all seated around her, hushed and expectant. She carried on for a while ignoring us, and then we became the focal point of her attention. She gaze, examined, explored us, and finally she chose the person that her ancestors called. It was James! Ralph said that she did her best work with addicts, freed them from the demons, or dark spirits that held them, in a dance-like fight. It was strange, but I had never thought of James as an addict. True, he drank often, true his behaviour had hurt me, but all along I had never identified him that way. Knowing this made me sigh with relief. It wasn't about me. Addicts tend to hurt people because they cannot maintain the masks that they wear; they sneak away to the caverns of drink. James seemed reluctant to join in. After all, what was he doing at the Grotes? But she held onto him, pulling him, guiding him to her healing circle. She still didn't let go of him, but held his wrist tightly, and started to dance, first almost as if she was at a disco, but then everything went a bit crazy. James fell on the floor and she threw herself on top of him, writhing and moaning. It looked sexual for a while and I was a bit embarrassed. But then as though the wind changed, the atmosphere dulled, and the sound of a deep mummer echoed around the Grotes. I wasn't sure who was making the sound, but James no longer seemed to be pulling away or fighting. They seemed to be one being, and the deep murmuring sounded sub-human. Then James became very still and the shaman started dancing around the cave, around us in a wild frightening way, other shamans moved closer as if something dark and dangerous might occur, she danced for ages, perhaps two hours, and we all were exhausted, such was the intensity. Then James woke up sobbing, crying, then she held him tightly as though she were his mother, and we in turn turned to our neighbour and hugged each other.

Rosa   Afterwards I looked for Ralph. I wanted to talk with him about what I had just been part of. He was lying outside in the sunshine, he looked so beautiful. I sat next to him, and saw him look tired.
"I am both moved and drained", he said, "and you?"
"I am ecstatic. Wildly happy. I have just seen someone who I loved healed".
"Perhaps you should go and find them".
"I'd much rather be with you".
"And I'd much rather be with you", he said and we laughed.
"Strange", "We really hardly know each other".

Rosa   "But I know that I really like you and would not want to change you." That's a beautiful kind of love. Accepting someone as they are. Most of us love in a way that we would like to change the other person. It means taking your time getting to know each other, and not using alcohol to speed the process. But untangling the meaning from the words. Being alone, being still, being separate, and then being together and noticing the difference. We held hands as we lay under the tree, watching the light change and the tree breathe, its leaves swaying. And I have to say all anxiety left me. Nothing mattered but that moment - the azure blue sky, the cumulous clouds, the movement of the tree, its shadows on the floor, and the weight of each other's hands.

Nothing happened quickly between Ralph and me. It didn't make sense, to love fiercely and bright, when we both knew some many unhappy love stories. If love is balanced right it hovers in the atmosphere balanced on time, eternal...eternally, and that's what we were aiming for.

Sex and desire

Eva   Last night the television in the background provided the backdrop for a reminiscence of sorts. The grand historian talked about Henry VIII and Anne Boleyn and described their relationship as one of the epic love stories of all time. I studied Henry VIII time and time again, so much so that he began to represent history for a while, but I had never considered what happened between him and Anne Boleyn as a love story.

I saw the whole, not the chase, not the nine years of trying to be wed, but the whole, and more powerful in that whole was the fact that he murdered his so-called love: he chopped off her head. Last year in the summer my so-called illness made me feel the life of Anne, I even made a dress in the manner that she would have and went to church and bowed and waited as though my head would be chopped off, with all the intensity that it might happen. And now that I have experienced some of her I realise that for some love is just a chase, a game of wanting desiring, of grasping but never having. And should that having happen, should we be able to lie, twisted and held, and speak of, be together and find a stillness, the chase is lost, and the chase for some is the best part of love - as I grow nearer you pull away, as I pull away you grow nearer.

Rosa   We danced more, and the group became more united, our love for each other grew, but I began to see through the dance that Ralph didn't seem to love me any more than he loved anyone, and I was greatly disappointed. Again I felt that there was no one who wanted to be with me in a special and intimate way. When people formed unions of desire I felt excluded and also betrayed by God. Was I not one of the most Romantic people on the planet? Did I not offer the possibility of a grand love? I carried on being part of the group work, but would take any opportunity to be alone. To gather my thoughts, and hear the whisperings of my own mind. Again and again my mind repeated the same words, as though a mantra," I wish to be cherished'. Not for a while, and then have my head chopped off in anger and disappointment, forever, and ever, beyond time, through time forever and ever: To be loved in a glance, in a hug, in a conversation, in stillness. But how to step outside of the drama? Love and drama seemed to unite and be irrevocably connected, disturbing, turning, without space to breathe, to think, and then I would be dead or dying, thinking of regrets, of lost love, of whys and wherefores, of possibilities that never happened.

My mind might have seemed angry but I felt for the first time that I was connecting with it. True, it wasn't in a state of bliss- that was a state that I had felt when we first started to dance. It was in a state of healing, and I began to cry. I was healing, thank God I was healing, and with the tears my fears fell away. The conditioning fell away, and I began to see that I had a heavy gate around my being, impenetrable, keeping me safe, but also keeping everyone out, and I that I could now work to replace that gate with love. Unquestionable love, that was infinite and possible, and part of the continuum of being, not part of a power struggle.

Rosa   I closed my eyes and when I opened them I realised that Ralph's body was pressed next to mine. We stood still like this stillness inside the movement without doing anything. I felt that as he had moved close to me that the next move was mine, and I didn't know what to do! Usually I would have kissed a person, given this being an everyday occurrence. But I knew I didn't feel ready for something like that, and realised how many times I might have kissed out of expectation.

I didn't feel like anything sexual, or sensual, and I was so glad to know this about myself. Because I realised that whatever was happening with Ralph offered the possibility to keep my body, its desires and needs in check with the need of my mind; my being wanted to be known, far more than my mouth needed to be kissed, my cheek stroked, my hand held, my lips brushed, my tongue moistened- all these aspects of love-making shovelled and thrown at me again and again. So I just stood still, feeling still, awkward unsure but still until we moved apart and continued to dance. I realised I didn't have to move, like a series of chess moves, I had to listen to myself, and dancing with the music and the sounds of everyone else was giving me an opportunity to heal the side of myself that had to listen to me. And I realised I had started a process that was unknown. I had no idea where it would go, and I liked this.

Eva   As we came nearer and near to the end of my time at Illigruum house, I became aware that the only love I really wanted was a kind, spiritual cerebral caring one. That anything to do with sex made me cringe. Sex represented death, not life for me. The way someone looked on the crest of desire- their face misshapen and contorted. The rushing, the clumsiness- how so often people lacked grace and slowness, but rushed, pushed and pulled. Equally though I was scared to ask for something beautiful, touching and holding, caresses of loving without sex, and knowing this instead of changing myself, it might be time to just accept myself.

That actually there was nothing to achieve, that touch was not about achieving anything but about being. Will you sit with me and watch the rain fall from the grey sky softly hit the dull tarmac, listening only to the voices in our minds? That would be the greatest date. There was silence for a long while, as we realised that Rosa's stories had finished. We started to hug each other deeply and warmly, and spent our last evening with the rest of Illigruum House dancing, laughing, healing, and dancing some more. No more words, no more thinking, just love and love, and love.

Thanks to my son Jazz Manual and my partner Adam. Thanks also to Ralf and the 5 Rhythms Sanga. To my Mum Josephine, Dad Vivian, and sister Danielle, and also to the rest of my family, who have been very loving and accepting. Thanks also to my friends Nicole, Marta, Andrew Gadd and other Very lovely friends. Lastly thanks to the Basque part of our family.

www.ingramcontent.com/pod-product-compliance
Lightning Source LLC
Chambersburg PA
CBHW031215270326
41931CB00006B/574